I0030661

THE AI-DRIVEN INTERNAL AUDIT

THE AI-DRIVEN INTERNAL AUDIT

The AX Framework for Transforming Internal Audit in the AGI Era

Hiro Tsuchida

©2025 All Rights Reserved. No portion of this book may be reproduced, stored in a retrieval system, or transmitted in any form or by any means—electronic, mechanical, photocopy, recording, scanning, or other—except for brief quotations in critical reviews or articles without the prior permission of the author.

Published by Game Changer Publishing

Paperback ISBN: 978-1-962656-80-1
Hardcover ISBN: 978-1-968250-09-6
Digital ISBN: 978-1-968250-10-2

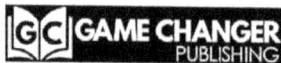

GAME CHANGER PUBLISHING

www.GameChangerPublishing.com

READ THIS FIRST

Thank you for buying and reading my book!

I'd love to connect with you and share ongoing insights and the latest developments about AI applications in Internal Audit and GRC.

Scan the QR code below to follow my IA Insight Lab,
where I regularly publish updates, opinions,
and thought leadership articles.

Scan the QR Code Here:

Stay ahead in the world of AI-driven Audit!

THE AI-DRIVEN INTERNAL AUDIT

The AX Framework for Transforming
Internal Audit in the AGI Era

Accelerate Assurance, Empower Governance with AI

Hiro Tsuchida

TABLE OF CONTENTS

INTRODUCTION

Thank you very much for picking up this book. In recent years, it has become increasingly evident that we are rapidly approaching an era where **Artificial General Intelligence (AGI)** will become commonplace, fundamentally reshaping the core of corporate operations. Beginning with the launch of ChatGPT in late 2022, generative AI technologies have continued to advance at an astonishing pace. Many experts now anticipate that **AGI will reach practical, widespread implementation by approximately 2030**. Looking even further ahead to around 2050, some scholars have raised the possibility of a technological singularity—a point at which AI may become capable of autonomously self-improving and self-evolving. This could lead to a future in which corporate decision-making and business processes are predominantly executed through interactions solely between AI agents—known as **AI-to-AI (A2A)** transactions.

In such a future environment, the conventional internal audit methodologies that have been human-centered—characterized by periodic audits on multi-year cycles, narrowly focused on selected areas based on assessed risk (hereafter referred to as **Rotational and Limited-Scope Auditing**)—will undoubtedly face severe limitations in both coverage and responsiveness. As AI autonomously handles massive volumes of transactions and contracts at extraordinary speeds, and even self-replicates to create entirely new business processes, internal audit functions will need to undergo a substantial transformation to avoid a situation in which critical emerging risks are overlooked.

This book addresses precisely **why the transformation of internal audit is necessary at this critical juncture** and outlines a clear roadmap for **how to effectively achieve this transformation**. Grounded in the original concept of **AX (AGI Transformation)**, it introduces a proprietary framework called **AXceleration (AX + Acceleration)** to systematically guide your organization's internal audit evolution. Even as AI continues its remarkable progression, potentially surpassing human intelligence, the core purpose and fundamental role of internal audit will not diminish. On the contrary, the importance of internal audit as the **last line of defense** will significantly intensify in the AGI era.

It is my sincere hope for this book to serve as a valuable resource for thoughtfully navigating and reinforcing your organization's corporate governance practices as we move forward together into the transformative AGI era.

1. MY CAREER AND THE PURPOSE OF THIS BOOK

1.1   A Holistic View of Management Through the Lens of Technology

To set the stage for this book, allow me to briefly introduce my own career background. I am currently based in Silicon Valley—often considered the epicenter of innovation in the contemporary world—where my professional activities are focused primarily on Governance, Risk management, and Compliance (GRC), as well as internal auditing. My work encompasses three core dimensions, detailed below. For clarity, GRC refers to the structures and processes through which companies maintain an appropriate internal control environment, manage risks effectively, and ensure sustainable growth. Internal auditing, meanwhile, denotes the independent and objective processes used to diagnose and evaluate these governance and risk management practices.

1. Business Executive and Management Consultant

At major global professional services firms, including PwC and Deloitte, I have supported diverse companies in implementing and enhancing their GRC frameworks and internal audit functions. Through these engagements, it became crystal clear that to drive meaningful transformation within an organization, it is essential to holistically address five interconnected areas: **methodology, culture, organizational structure, human resources, and technology**. Beyond my consulting roles, as an entrepreneur and executive leading my own ventures, I am continually putting these insights into practice.

2. Internal Auditor

I have conducted internal audits and business diagnostics for more than 100 companies across 15 countries. In executing these audits, I have consistently factored in international regulatory requirements, diverse cultural contexts, data utilization practices, and organizational dynamics. This comprehensive experience has deeply impressed upon me **the intrinsic value and excitement of internal auditing when closely aligned with business strategy**— to the extent that I often describe internal auditing as a personal passion and lifelong pursuit.

3. Engineer

My career originally began in engineering, where I gained hands-on experience in programming and systems development. These early experiences gave me profound insight into the transformative effect technology can have on both businesses and society as a whole. Today, this technical foundation fuels my drive for innovation within the fields of GRC and internal auditing. In Silicon Valley, I am actively involved in the development of software leveraging AI technologies, constantly exploring new ways to create additional value by integrating AI and internal audit functions.

By integrating these multi-dimensional perspectives—**management, auditing, technology, and global insights**—I have gained unique insights into organizational challenges. These experiences have led me to conclude with some confidence that we stand on the brink of an era in which AGI (artificial general intelligence) will become central to corporate operations. Consequently, it is clear to me that as executives and internal auditors, **we must urgently engage in fundamental reforms of corporate governance, particularly internal audit practices, to proactively address this impending shift**.

1.2 The Impact of the Evolution of Artificial General Intelligence (AGI)

Since the public release of ChatGPT at the end of 2022, generative AI has continued to evolve at an astonishing pace. Many experts predict that **AGI will reach practical application levels by around 2030**. Looking further ahead, by around 2050, it is anticipated that **AI-to-AI (A2A)** contracts and negotiations will become central to corporate operations, dramatically increasing business transactions conducted with minimal human intervention.

As someone intimately familiar with the realities of internal auditing, I firmly believe that traditional auditing methods—such as **Rotational and Limited-Scope Auditing** and **sampling-based testing**—pose a high risk of overlooking critical issues. In an environment characterized by massive volumes of A2A transactions occurring in real-time, it will become practically impossible to provide sufficient assurance through manual audits alone.

This acute awareness of the profound risks that lie ahead represented **the core motivation behind the writing of this book**.

2. THE CRITICAL ASSURANCE DEFICIT IN THE AGE OF AGI

2.1 AI Agents Becoming Black Boxes

As AGI becomes prevalent, internal business processes traditionally managed by humans—such as procurement, payments, and negotiations—will increasingly be replaced by automated interactions between AI agents. Each time new business processes emerge, AI will autonomously generate additional AI agents as needed, effectively self-replicating. In the future, we may realistically face a scenario often described as dystopian, where **AI oversees and manages other AI agents**.

In such an environment, traditional auditing methods will be grossly inadequate in terms of both coverage and speed. In a world where **AI-to-AI (A2A)** transactions enable instantaneous contract conclusions and settlements, human-centric methods like **Rotational and Limited-Scope Auditing** and sampling-based testing will very likely fail to identify risks occurring at high frequency and immense speed. This could very swiftly lead to severe reputational damage for businesses.

- **AI Automation of Internal Processes**

  With AI handling most internal processes—such as expense management, supplier selection, and HR administration—it will become increasingly difficult for humans to pinpoint precisely when and where fraud or errors occur.

- **AI Automation of External Transactions**

  When AIs from different corporations autonomously execute A2A contracts and settlements, transaction volumes will skyrocket. Sampling-based audits will therefore pose a significantly higher risk of failing to detect critical issues.

2.2 Limitations of Human-Centric Auditing Methods

Traditional internal auditing approaches typically involve **rotationally selecting audit targets on a periodic basis** within an annual audit plan, **significantly limiting the audit scope based on risk**, and then **conducting sample-based verification**. Such an approach has long been considered standard practice. Given the constraints of human resources, this risk-based methodology was indeed highly effective.

However, in the era of AGI, these conventional approaches encounter critical limitations:

- **Increased Likelihood of Overlooking Critical Risks**

  In an AGI-driven environment characterized by a massive escalation in risks, auditing even just 10 out of 100 locations annually—extracting mere dozens of samples from millions of transactions—will lead to extremely low coverage and exponentially increase the likelihood of missing significant risks.

- **Rapidly Escalating Volume and Speed of Transactions Due to A2A**

  With AI agents executing contracts and payments within milli-seconds, any human-led retrospective checks will inevitably lag far behind, rendering responses significantly delayed and ineffective.

- **The Proliferation of Sophisticated AI-Driven Fraud Attacks**

  AI agents collaborating on cyberattacks and similar fraud tactics will become commonplace. Such highly sophisticated attacks will render human auditors virtually incapable of discerning the truth.

The fundamental misalignment between human-centric auditing methods and this new environment precisely encapsulates what we identify as **the Critical Assurance Deficit of the AGI era**.

3. THE IMPERATIVE SHIFT TOWARD NEXT-GENERATION AUDITING— AI-DRIVEN AUDIT

3.1 Positioning AI at the Core of Internal Auditing

The key to overcoming the Critical Assurance Deficit lies in funda-mentally rethinking the role of AI—not merely as a supplementary tool, but as **the central pillar of the auditing function**. This strategic shift entails the introduction of what we call the **AI Auditor.** By boldly revising traditional methods limited by human resources and sampling-based testing, organizations can fully leverage AI auditors to deliver assurance at a level previously unimaginable to management.

- **Comprehensive Expansion of the Audit Scope (Full-Scope Auditing)**

  AI auditors can instantaneously analyze massive volumes of data, overcoming human resource limitations. **For instance, an organi-zation previously limited to auditing 10 sites annually can now simultaneously cover all 100 sites.**

- **Real-Time Monitoring**

  AI can automatically analyze every transaction as it occurs, immediately alerting audit departments and executive management upon detecting anomalies. Rather than post-event checks, **real-time monitoring becomes the new norm**.

3.2 Enhancing the Strategic Value of Internal Audit Through the AI Auditor

With AI auditors performing routine assurance tasks—such as standardized testing, evidence collection, and compliance checks—human auditors can concentrate their efforts on more sophisticated and value-adding activities, notably **consulting engagements**, improvement proposals, and strategic advisory roles.

The fundamental message of this book is that the AGI era presents internal auditors with an unprecedented opportunity to become deeply embedded in strategic decision-making. Internal auditors will not merely uncover irregularities; instead, they will actively support business strategy through a risk-focused lens, ultimately positioning themselves as **Trusted Advisors** to the organization's leadership.

4. PROPOSALS FOR INTERNAL AUDIT REFORM IN THE AGI ERA

4.1 Why Internal Audit Must Transform: Understanding AX

As AGI becomes increasingly widespread, business activities will shift toward AI-to-AI (A2A) transactions, dramatically escalating both the volume and velocity of risks. Maintaining traditional audit models will inevitably lead to failure. Thus, a fundamental update toward an AI-driven internal audit is imperative.

The concept of **AX (AGI Transformation)** proposed in this book is designed to comprehensively reform internal auditing by leveraging AI to adapt to this rapidly evolving business environment. **AX positions internal audit to become a strategic partner for business management**, fundamentally enhancing its role within the organization.

4.2 A Roadmap for Advancing AX: Introducing the AXceleration Framework

To effectively implement AX, this book presents the original **AXceleration (AX + Acceleration)** framework. By combining the five elements

(MCOST) with five implementation stages (AEPIE), the framework provides a structured path toward holistic and phased governance reform, avoiding partial optimization.

MCOST: The Five Core Elements

- **Methodology**

  Boldly transitioning from traditional **Rotational and Limited-Scope Auditing** to **Full-Scope Real-Time Auditing**.

- **Culture**

  Cultivating an organizational mindset that views AI as a partner rather than a threat, fostering an **AI-friendly culture** that welcomes early detection of issues and proactive improvements.

- **Organization**

  Structuring global teams, such as AI Audit Teams and Consulting Enhancement Teams, to manage GRC (Governance, Risk Management, Compliance) at scale, balancing independence and collaboration across the global enterprise.

- **Skillset**

  Developing **hybrid auditors** who possess foundational GRC expertise, advanced AI literacy, consulting proficiencies, and strategic business insight through continuous reskilling and professional development.

- **Technology**

  Establishing a robust AI Audit Platform and comprehensive data infrastructure to facilitate automation and real-time auditing, while rigorously managing security risks.

AEPIE: The Five Implementation Stages

- **Assess** (Current State Assessment)

  Conduct a comprehensive evaluation of the MCOST elements, clearly identifying current assurance gaps, and performing a thorough Fit & Gap analysis against the desired audit model for the AGI era.

- **Envision** (Vision Development)

  Clearly define the objectives for **Full-Scope Real-Time Auditing**, formalize them into an AX strategic roadmap, and secure executive agreement.

- **Pilot** (Pilot Implementation)

  Begin with a limited-scale pilot to demonstrate quick wins, systematically addressing resistance within the organization, and gradually expanding AI-Driven Audit.

- **Implement** (Full-Scale Implementation)

  Scale the AX initiative globally and across the entire organization, elevating AI-Driven Audit as standard operational practice and embedding a new audit process tailored for the AGI era.

- **Elevate** (Continuous Improvement)

  Persistently refine and advance all MCOST elements. Implement robust **AI Model Auditing** to ensure bias-free, reliable operations of the AI Auditor, cementing trust in AI-Driven Audit processes.

4.3   The Value Delivered by AX Through AI-Driven Audit

- **Delivering Exponentially Greater Assurance to Management**

  Through **Full-Scope Real-Time Auditing**, organizations will be able to proactively detect and prevent fraud or errors early on. Coverage, once limited, will be dramatically expanded, exponentially increasing the assurance provided.

- **Establishing the Internal Auditor as a Trusted Advisor**

  With AI auditors taking on routine assurance tasks, human auditors will be able to transition their focus to higher-value consulting engagements, improvement recommendations, and strategic advisory roles, thereby actively contributing to corporate value enhancement.

- **Elevating the Career Value of Internal Auditors**

  Internal auditors equipped with both AI literacy and consulting expertise will gain increased recognition as future-oriented auditors who possess a strategic, global business perspective. The internal audit department can thus become a key stepping-stone for future business leaders.

5. STRUCTURE OF THIS BOOK AND INTENDED AUDIENCE

5.1 Structure of This Book

- **Chapter 1: The Future Journey of Internal Audit—GlobalCorp's AX Story (2050)**

  This chapter paints a vivid, science-fiction-inspired narrative of internal auditors and AI auditors working collaboratively in a post-AGI world of 2050, providing readers a glimpse into the future of internal auditing after the widespread adoption of AGI.

- **Chapter 2: The Dawn of the AGI Era in 2030**

  This chapter offers a detailed exploration of the business environment in 2030, clearly illustrating why internal auditing must undergo a significant transformation in response to the emergence of AGI.

- **Chapter 3: Overview of the AX Framework—AXceleration**

  In this chapter, readers will gain a comprehensive understanding of the AXceleration framework, including its theoretical foundations and overall structure, serving as the backbone of AX implementation.

- **Chapters 4–8: Deep Dive into the AXceleration Framework**

  These chapters provide an in-depth exploration of each of the five AXceleration stages—Assess, Envision, Pilot, Implement, and Elevate (AEPIE)—with practical guidance from the MCOST perspective (Methodology, Culture, Organization, Skillset, Technology).

- **Chapter 9: A Case Study of AGI Transformation (AX) in Internal Audit—The AX Journey of GlobalCorp (2025–2030)**

  A detailed fictional narrative spanning the period 2025–2030 demonstrates how internal auditors at GlobalCorp successfully applied the AX framework in practice, highlighting real-world insights and experiences.

- **Chapter 10: Conclusion and the Path Ahead—Taking AX to the Next Level**

  This final chapter summarizes the key messages of the book, reiterating critical points of the AX framework and offering a compelling vision for the future of internal auditing in the AGI era.

5.2 Intended Audience for This Book

- **Senior Management (e.g., CEO/CFO/CRO)**

  Executives leading governance, risk management, and internal control initiatives at the highest levels, particularly those preparing their organizations for the AGI era.

- **Chief Audit Executives (CAEs), Audit Managers, and Internal Audit Staff**

  Leaders and practitioners within internal audit functions who seek practical insights into implementing AI-driven transformations within their departments.

- **Governance, Risk, and Compliance (GRC) Professionals**

  Experts involved in AI implementation or Digital Transformation (DX) initiatives who are exploring comprehensive governance reform as part of their strategic roadmap.

- **Professionals at Global Companies**

  Individuals responsible for managing overseas subsidiaries and navigating complex international regulatory environments who face unique governance and compliance challenges.

6. THE INDISPENSABLE ROLE OF INTERNAL AUDIT IN THE AGI ERA

The era of AGI will fundamentally reshape corporate activities. While this transition will undoubtedly bring significant risks, it also represents an extraordinary opportunity to dramatically expand the role and importance of internal auditing. By shifting internal audit toward an **AI-Driven Audit** model, organizations can realize innovative new approaches such as **Full-Scope Real-Time Auditing**. Internal auditors will be empowered to shift their focus from mere compliance checking to providing strategic consulting services—including proactive recommendations and insightful management advice—thus solidifying their role as **Trusted Advisors** and directly contributing to greater corporate value.

Some may still hold the perception that internal auditing is inherently mundane or overly technical. However, the reality is quite the opposite: internal auditing now stands at the exciting intersection of management, audit, and cutting-edge technology. This book captures this emerging potential in the concept of **AX (AGI Transformation)** and provides a clear, structured framework—**AXceleration (AX + Acceleration)**—to guide you through the necessary steps to fully harness this potential.

As you delve deeper into each chapter, I encourage you to vividly imagine how your organization and your career can evolve by adopting the AX framework. Embracing AX means your organization can confidently navigate the complexities of the AGI era, achieving a balance between proactive risk management (**defensive auditing**) and strategic business growth (**proactive auditing**). Conversely, hesitation or failure to adapt could leave your organization confined by outdated methodologies, exposing it to severe risks of compliance failures, scandals, and declining competitiveness.

Far from diminishing, the role of internal auditing in the AGI era has the potential to expand significantly. It is my sincere hope that the framework and roadmap provided in this book will serve as practical guidance and inspiration, helping you and your organization to successfully navigate the transformative years ahead, and thrive in the exciting era they will bring. Thank you for joining me on this journey; I look forward to guiding you through the chapters that follow.

CHAPTER 1

The Future Journey of Internal Audit— GlobalCorp's AX Story (2050)

— Internal Auditors and AI Auditors Navigating a Post-AGI World —

INTRODUCTION: WHY WE ARE DEPICTING A WORLD 25 YEARS FROM NOW

Why are we opening this book by vividly depicting a world 25 years into the future, in the year 2050? It is because **imagining and visualizing the future enables us to work backward to today, making the upcoming risks and opportunities posed by AGI tangible and relatable for readers**.

The scenario of rapid AGI proliferation and the corresponding explosive growth of AI-to-AI (A2A) transactions is already predicted by numerous experts to become mainstream in the 2030s. For example, consider a world where AI agents autonomously execute contracts, manage instantaneous payments, and handle logistics without human intervention.

This is no longer mere science fiction. When AI becomes integral to the core of corporate activities, transactions, and processes that no longer require human decision-making will drastically increase. Eventually, AI systems may autonomously create new AI entities, with central AI systems ("Central AIs") managing a multitude of AI agents and orchestrating entire corporate operations. Such a structure may very well become commonplace.

Yet, **this future is by no means a dystopia**. Human internal auditors will still be present, collaborating closely with AI auditors to continuously monitor risks and proactively provide new value to management.

Some readers may understandably feel that 25 years from now seems too distant to comprehend—not least given the dizzying rates of chance we currently experience in most areas of our lives. However, by working backward from the roadmap presented in this book, you'll recognize that **actions taken today can lead to dramatically different outcomes as early as the 2030s**. In this chapter, we intentionally present a seemingly distant, extraordinary scenario—internal auditing in 2050—and demonstrate that this vision is entirely plausible. By doing so, readers will be able to vividly grasp the urgency and excitement of AI, making the implications personally relevant.

1.1. A Day in 2050, When AGI Has Become the Norm

9:00 AM: GlobalCorp Headquarters, Where a Holographic AI Auditor Works

The year is 2050. On the 48th floor of GlobalCorp's towering headquarters in Silicon Valley, the elevator opens onto an expansive lobby filled with holographic displays projecting interactive, floating art, creating a surreal and captivating ambiance. Outside panoramic windows, countless drone taxis and aerial vehicles traverse the sky in dense, multi-layered traffic, signaling that even congestion has transitioned from ground level to the skies. It is commonplace to see humans casually conversing with humanoid robots, which effortlessly carry their luggage or supplies. Indeed, Silicon Valley in 2050 epitomizes an advanced future metropolis where humans and AI coexist seamlessly.

At the center of the floor is a circular control desk. When Mei Sakamoto, the leader of the **AI Audit Team**, places her hand over the desk, a palm-sized hologram gently emerges, greeting her calmly:

"Good morning, Mei. Since last night, we've detected 124 new risk alerts. The inventory discrepancy at the North American facility appears to be most critical. How would you like to proceed?"

The voice belongs to **Axel**, an AI Auditor integrated with GlobalCorp's **Central AI**. Within this corporation, tens of thousands of **AI-to-AI (A2A)** transactions occur every minute. The Central AI continuously orchestrates numerous autonomously generated AI agents, automatically managing complex, interconnected operations. Axel's critical role is constant monitoring of these immense operations, swiftly identifying and isolating risks. Audit cycles, formerly conducted merely several times annually, have now evolved into real-time, second-by-second monitoring and instant reporting, immediately visualized on the **Global AI Audit Cockpit (Dashboard)**.

"Thanks, Axel," Mei responds promptly. "Let's prioritize that North American inventory issue. Show me more details on my AR screen."

Instantly, a 3D augmented reality projection appears on Mei's AR glasses, clearly marking the precise locations and timestamps of the inventory discrepancies, highlighted vividly in red and yellow. Auditing in 2050 feels worlds away from the practices of the past, when audit teams visited physical locations burdened with stacks of paper documentation and manual checklists.

10:00 AM: Remote Audit via VR Booth

Mei steps into a translucent capsule-shaped booth equipped with advanced AR/VR functionalities, activating the mode for virtual travel to any global location. Within mere seconds, a vivid, 360-degree panoramic view of the massive warehouse in GlobalCorp's North American factory surrounds her, creating an authentic sense of being physically present.

Inside the warehouse, robotic forklifts and humanoid workers move efficiently under precise instructions from the Central AI. Very few human supervisors are present; the vast majority of transactions and inventory transfers are autonomously conducted through AI-to-AI agreements and directives.

Axel promptly informs Mei, **"Mei, here's the shelf causing the inventory discrepancy. According to the A2A transaction logs, the inconsistency arose around 8:15 AM this morning."**

"Thank you, Axel. Analyze the behavior of the AI counterpart involved in the transaction. If necessary, I'll speak directly with the responsible human manager," Mei replies calmly.

Auditing in 2050 operates under the established principle that **"AI continuously gathers audit data,"** allowing human auditors to **"drill deeply into specific issues only when needed."** By tracing the shelf's 3D representation with her fingertips, Mei swiftly identifies which AI agent authorized inventory movements, reviewing nearly real-time inventory transfer logs from the past 24 hours. A few decades ago, an investigation of this depth might have taken weeks. Today, it typically takes mere minutes.

11:00 AM: Detecting Fraudulent Signatures and Immediate Response to the European Office

Suddenly, Axel's voice echoes urgently:

"A cyberattack orchestrated by an AI agent has been detected. A supply chain contract at our European office appears to have been

tampered with. Fraudulent signatures have been identified within the blockchain-based smart contracts."

If this tampering spreads significantly, it could potentially result in millions of dollars in losses and severely damage trust. However, with auditing built around AI in 2050, such incidents are detected almost immediately upon occurrence. Mei quickly instructs Axel, **"Set up an immediate online meeting with the European team."** Within minutes, Mei engages with the local team through a VR conference, swiftly coordinating their response. Even in a business environment characterized by ultra-fast **AI-to-AI (A2A)** transactions, **Full-Scope Real-Time Auditing** ensures that any damages are minimized to the greatest extent possible—this is the fundamental advantage of auditing in 2050.

1:00 PM: Real-Time Reporting to Executive Management

After lunch, an online board meeting takes place. Mei quickly reviews and summarizes Axel's dashboard insights in just ten minutes, clearly explaining that **"The North American inventory discrepancy resulted from a misunderstanding in shelf restocking processes,"** and that **"The fraudulent signatures in Europe were resolved immediately following detection."** Board members and the CEO now receive instantaneous updates on risk conditions without having to wait for annual or even quarterly audit reports. If additional decisions are required, these can be made in a matter of a few hours.

While internal auditing used to be limited to post-event checks, reported quarterly or annually, by 2050, it has evolved into a continuously active, real-time operation. Thus, the evolution into **Full-Scope Real-Time Auditing** now actively underpins corporate management around the clock.

3:00 PM: Choosing a Physical Visit for Human Insight

Later in the afternoon, Mei boards a drone shuttle to physically visit the North American factory. Although VR and holographic technologies provide considerable insight, Mei still feels the necessity of **"experiencing the real atmosphere on-site as a human."** Additionally, local staff expressed, **"We'd appreciate your presence here at least once,"** and Mei acknowledges the importance of such requests.

Looking out the window of the ascending drone shuttle, she sees countless aerial vehicles cross paths. Technology appears to have advanced to near perfection compared to half a century ago, yet Mei knows that there remains implicit human knowledge, perceptible only through human intuition. Even when AI seems flawless, human auditors continue to hold the critical responsibility of sensing organizational culture, employee morale, and local practices. They identify and address the subtle risks that AI alone cannot fully capture. Mei is deeply convinced that even in the world of 2050, the value of human auditors has, if anything, increased.

1.2. The Tragedy of a Former Competitor: The Consequences of Rejecting AX Implementation

What happened to **OldWays Corporation**, once considered a formidable rival to GlobalCorp? Despite similar revenue scales, OldWays' executive team dismissed the idea of **AI-Driven Audit**, arguing, *"It's merely an expensive overhead,"* and chose to persist with their traditional, human-led approach of **Rotational and Limited-Scope Auditing** and sampling-based testing. They failed to confront the rapidly increasing volume of **AI-to-AI (A2A)** transactions head-on. Consequently, by the 2030s, OldWays faced an escalating wave of fraud and scandals, and by 2050, rumors were circulating widely about the drastic decline of their corporate value.

Auditing Unable to Keep Pace with AI Transactions

Although OldWays partially introduced AI into some business areas, they remained heavily reliant on human-driven sampling-based testing. Firmly believing that checking every single transaction was impossible, they consistently postponed investing in AI-Driven Audit. As a result, numerous transactions at multiple locations piled up unchecked, allowing potential fraud and errors to remain hidden.

Series of Scandals and the Collapse of Corporate Value

When scandals inevitably surfaced, the reputational damage far exceeded expectations. Investors and business partners quickly withdrew, causing stock prices to plummet. Directors were held personally accountable, and amid the subsequent restructuring and business downsizing, the executives could only regretfully acknowledge, *"If only we had implemented a system like AX sooner."* Tragically, the price they paid for rejecting AI-Driven Audit proved devastatingly high.

1.3. The Shape of Auditing in the AGI Era

The contrasting paths of GlobalCorp and OldWays Corporation clearly illustrate a critical point: **Integrating AI into the core of auditing profoundly influences corporate destiny.** As **Artificial General Intelligence (AGI)** and **AI-to-AI (A2A)** transactions become commonplace, traditional **Rotational and Limited-Scope Auditing** conducted by human auditors becomes insufficient, inevitably leading to assurance gaps. Conversely, standardizing **Full-Scope Real-Time Auditing**, driven by AI to comprehensively and immediately capture risks, not only enhances fraud detection but transforms auditing into a proactive force supporting strategic management.

- **Full-Scope Auditing**

  This approach thoroughly covers critical risks and controls across every process in every location. It moves away from sampling-based testing, significantly reducing the risk of undetected fraud or misconduct occurring outside traditional auditing scopes.

- **Real-Time Auditing**

  Rather than relying on scheduled annual or quarterly audits, AI continuously monitors each transaction, immediately generating alerts upon detecting abnormalities. By establishing mechanisms for immediate reporting and responsive action, potential damages can be greatly mitigated.

- **Human–AI Collaboration Model in Auditing**

  In this collaboration, AI auditors handle verification, monitoring, and other assurance-related tasks, while human auditors concentrate on consulting activities, including providing strategic advice and improvement recommendations. Together, they achieve a powerful synergy capable of addressing emerging risks in the AGI era.

The year 2050 vividly illustrates the evolution of auditing: **from a peripheral corporate function to an integral partner in strategic management.** Far from a dystopia or a world where human auditors become obsolete, it is a future where auditors who skillfully harness AI define success. **This transformative partnership between human insight and AI efficiency lies at the heart of this narrative.**

KEY TAKEAWAYS FROM THIS CHAPTER

- **AI-Driven Audit will be essential by 2050, the age of AGI**

  In an era when millions of **AI-to-AI (A2A)** transactions occur instantaneously to drive corporate operations, **Full-Scope Real-Time Auditing** powered by AI is essential to provide adequate assurance to management.

- **Collaboration between human auditors and AI auditors significantly enhances the value of internal audit**

  While AI continuously monitors transactions, human auditors focus their efforts on consulting, thus simultaneously mitigating risks and supporting strategic management to enhance corporate value.

- **Implementing AX before 2030 will create a decisive competitive advantage**

  Organizations that fail to proactively adopt **AX (AGI Transformation)** prior to the widespread adoption of AGI and A2A transactions around 2030 will risk overlooking critical fraud incidents and experiencing significant erosion of corporate value. Conversely, firms that embrace AX early will gain a decisive competitive edge.

LOOKING AHEAD TO THE NEXT CHAPTER:
THE TIME FOR AX IS NOW

The vision of the year 2050 depicted in this chapter might appear science-fictional at first glance. However, considering that many experts predict **AI agents will handle the majority of business activities by around 2030**, this future is closer than we realize. Organizations that fail to initiate AX now and continue relying on traditional methods such as **Rotational and Limited-Scope Auditing** or sampling-based testing may face situations like OldWays Corporation—where fraudulent transactions buried within unmonitored data or sophisticated cyberattacks are detected far too late to take effective action.

On the other hand, companies like GlobalCorp, which firmly establish a foundation of AI-driven **Full-Scope Real-Time Auditing** centered around "AI auditors" by 2025, will by 2030 be well-equipped to roll out proactive auditing globally. Such companies lay the groundwork for a robust auditing infrastructure, empowering auditors to practice "proactive auditing" consistently. By 2050, as exemplified by Mei's role, it will be commonplace to see auditors collaborating seamlessly with AI to lead corporate governance.

In the next chapter, we shift our focus to a more realistic perspective: examining the business landscape of 2030 and the urgent need for transformation within internal auditing. The chapter will identify critical priorities in the years leading up to the widespread adoption of A2A transactions and clarify the rationale and overall vision required to effectively implement AX.

The future illustrated by the year 2050 clearly demonstrates how **proactive auditing, in collaboration with AI**, can significantly accelerate business growth. This vision is within reach for every organization willing to take that initial step now. My sincere hope is that through reading this book, you will embark on your organization's own "AX journey," ensuring your internal audit function not only survives but thrives and actively drives growth in the era of transformative change.

CHAPTER 2
The Dawn of the AGI Era in 2030

*—The Changing Business Environment and the Urgent Need
for Internal Audit Transformation—*

INTRODUCTION: 2030 AS A CRITICAL TURNING POINT

In the previous chapter, I illustrated the future landscape of 2050 in a speculative, science-fictional style scenario, helping you envision a society in
which **Artificial General Intelligence (AGI)** has become deeply integrated,
and **AI-Driven Audit** plays a central role. In that world, massive volumes
of high-speed **AI-to-AI (A2A)** transactions are commonplace, and human
auditors work closely with AI auditors, playing a vital role in supporting
business operations.

However, if we simply watch the journey unfold toward 2050 without taking
action, we risk overlooking the turbulent changes that are already upon us.
In reality, the year **2030** is likely to mark a critical tipping point for us. Many
experts anticipate that **AGI will see practical implementation and significantly impact corporate activities throughout the 2030s**.

In just a few short years, ultra-high-speed transactions and real-time settlements between AI entities (A2A transactions) will become standard business
practices. When this happens, traditional auditing methods such as Rotational
and Limited-Scope Auditing or sampling-based checks will no longer be sufficient to effectively cover the sheer volume of transactions. This situation will
sharply increase the risk of overlooking serious fraud or errors.

Therefore, this chapter will delve into the following crucial topics:

- **Why 2030 represents a critical turning point**
- **How the explosion of A2A transactions will transform businesses,
  and what implications this holds for internal auditing**
- **Why the transition to AI-Driven Audit is both urgent and promising**

I want to emphasize a dual perspective: If we fail to act starting from 2030, we
risk facing severe scandals and financial losses that could emerge suddenly
and dramatically. On the other hand, proactively adopting AI-Driven Audit can

successfully balance defensive and offensive strategies, potentially driving significant enhancement in corporate value.

2.1 Business in 2030: The Era of Routine AI-to-AI (A2A) Transactions

(1) Accelerating Automation and the Massive Wave of A2A

Many corporations have already integrated Robotic Process Automation (RPA) and machine learning into their operations, making automation of routine tasks practically commonplace. However, we anticipate that, by around 2030, we will enter the next stage: where **AI-to-AI (A2A)** transactions will become mainstream.

Consider the following scenarios, which may soon be common within corporate environments:

- **Entire supply chains will be interconnected through AI**. For example, demand forecasting AI identifies a "20% increase in sales expected next week," immediately prompting procurement AI to automatically place orders with supplier AI.

- **Contracts will become smart contracts**, with instantaneous agreements executed via blockchain. By the time a human manager clicks an approval button, the actual transaction might already be completed.

- **In financial markets**, AI traders will negotiate and set prices within nanoseconds, repeatedly executing trades. Humans will merely review results after the fact.

Initially, these **A2A transactions** may be introduced partially or experimentally. Yet, by 2030, they could become remarkably widespread, since AI-driven decision-making operates at speeds and parallel-processing capabilities far beyond human limitations. To maintain competitive advantage, companies will have little choice but to adopt such technology proactively.

- **Supply Chains**:

  Procurement AI linked directly with predictive sales AI will autonomously optimize inventory. Without human intervention, the complete cycle from contracting and payment through to shipment will proceed automatically.

- **Finance and Investment**:

  While high-frequency trading (HFT) is already a reality today, future AI will autonomously handle everything from risk assessment and negotiation to designing complex derivatives. Human traders may not even have the chance to witness major financial movements in real-time.

- **Internal Operations**:

  AI agents will autonomously approve expense reimbursements, employee performance evaluations, and other operational decisions, consulting each other as necessary. Humans will intervene only in exceptional cases, creating a potential scenario where operational processes might run unchecked by human oversight for extended periods.

With such an overwhelming wave of A2A transactions, auditing faces significant challenges in detecting risks and fraud. It is glaringly obvious that traditional approaches, such as visiting locations once every few years or sampling 25 transactions, will be insufficient to cover transaction volumes of this scale and speed.

(2) Speed that Transcends Human Decision-Making Cycles

As A2A transactions become standard, human decision-making speeds will never catch up to the microsecond-level AI interactions. This high-speed operational environment will extend beyond financial markets into production and manufacturing sectors as well.

- **Sampling Audits Will Become Meaningless:**

  When millions of contracts are transacted between AI systems, auditors sampling a few dozen transactions will inevitably fall behind. By the time the sampled audit results are finalized, thousands of new contracts will already have been executed, making the audit instantly obsolete.

- **Post-Facto Audit Will Already Be Too Late:**

  If an AI malfunction or fraudulent algorithm triggers unauthorized transactions, causing billions of dollars in losses, relying solely on quarterly or annual audits for detection will be catastrophic. By the time auditors uncover the issues months later, the company might already have suffered irreparable damage.

- **Only Full-Scope Real-Time Auditing Can Mitigate These Risks:**

  Ultimately, the only way to effectively monitor the constant stream of A2A transactions without gaps is by implementing **Full-Scope Real-Time Auditing**, ensuring every transaction is continuously monitored, and risks or anomalies are addressed immediately upon detection.

(3) Increasingly Black-Boxed Decision-Making Logic

It is not only the speed of A2A transactions that complicates auditing—AI decision-making itself is increasingly becoming an opaque "black box," difficult for humans to comprehend.

- **Unexplainability in Deep Learning and Reinforcement Learning:**

  In large-scale neural networks, decision-making logic is embedded across countless parameters, making it challenging—even for developers—to fully explain how or why a certain decision was made.

- **Self-Reinforcing Biases:**

  In environments where multiple AIs feed learning results back and forth, biases or incorrect assumptions can rapidly magnify. Without regular human oversight, serious fraud or discriminatory practices could remain undetected and escalate significantly.

- **Regulatory and Societal Pressures:**

  Regulations such as the EU AI Act increasingly require organizations to demonstrate and explain AI-driven decisions to some extent. Companies neglecting this black-box issue may expose themselves to compliance risks and societal backlash.

Considering these factors, auditing functions will inevitably require not only introducing **AI auditors** but also implementing dedicated measures such as **AI Model Auditing** and explainability frameworks (**Explainable AI**) to systematically review and verify AI models, even while embracing the surge of A2A transactions.

2.2 Limitations of Traditional Auditing Approaches

(1) Limitations of Rotational and Limited-Scope Auditing and Sampling-based Testing

In traditional internal auditing, the prevailing methodology has been, "Given limited resources, prioritize high-risk locations or processes and conduct deep dives through sampling." However, the fundamental assumptions behind this methodology become highly unstable in a future where A2A transactions accelerate.

- **Gap in Rotational Audit Cycles**

  For instance, while auditors visit various locations every few years in a rotational manner, **AI agents might execute tens of thousands of transactions daily across all global locations**. Locations not audited during the first year, left unchecked until the second or third year, are at risk of significant fraud and compliance breaches accumulating undetected.

- **Human-Dependent Sampling Falls Short**

  In an environment characterized by A2A transactions, **billions of contracts could be executed within extremely short periods**. Spending several days to sample a mere handful of transactions inevitably means conditions will change dramatically in the interim. Serious issues occurring outside the selected sample would remain unnoticed, causing delayed detection and exacerbating the potential impact.

(2) Risks of Ignoring the AI Decision-Making "Black Box"

Human-centric auditing traditionally emphasizes methods such as conducting interviews with responsible individuals or checking sampled documents and system logs. Yet, in AI-driven transactions, auditors will frequently encounter scenarios where there are no such **suitable interviewees**. When AI agents autonomously enter into contracts or self-modify algorithms, it becomes highly challenging for humans to grasp the underlying rationale of these decisions.

- **Absence of Interviewees**

  Traditional audits gain significant insights through interviews with responsible personnel. However, when AI exclusively makes decisions, the scenario transforms into one where no human counterpart is available (or, at best, only AI-generated logs exist). This situation requires auditors to possess specialized expertise in **AI Model Auditing** and log analytics.

· **Hotbed for Errors and Biases**

Incorrect data or faulty algorithms fed into AI systems, left unchecked, can become reinforced through autonomous learning, leading to considerable consequences before corrective actions can be effectively implemented.

(3) Misalignment with International Regulatory Frameworks

By 2030, various countries will likely implement increasingly stringent regulations related to AI. Regulatory frameworks, including the **EU AI Act** and data protection laws enacted by individual U.S. states, may significantly complicate compliance efforts. Under these circumstances, auditing only select locations or relying on limited sampling audits will no longer sustain integrated governance, dramatically increasing risks associated with regulatory noncompliance and potentially posing substantial penalties.

· **Heightened Risk for Global Corporations**

When regulatory compliance for AI across diverse regions is evaluated merely through limited or selective audits, corporations face substantial issues later on, potentially discovering that overseas operations were persistently non-compliant.

· **Requirement for Algorithm Transparency**

High-risk AI systems will increasingly be mandated to guarantee "explainability." With limited-scope audits, auditors risk failing to identify core algorithms promptly, potentially resulting in prolonged regulatory violations.

As international regulatory frameworks intersect with the burgeoning A2A transactional world, it will become essential to adopt comprehensive, real-time monitoring and auditing systems, and these are an inevitable foreseeable development. Hence, **AI-Driven Audit** will become necessary, capable of covering **every location, every process, and every risk in real-time**.

2.3   Shifting to Next-Generation Auditing: Implementing AI-Driven Audit

(1) Why AI Auditing of AI is Essential

As AI-to-AI (A2A) transactions become commonplace, the core of auditing will shift toward continuously monitoring and validating **massive amounts of data generated and managed by AI**, as well as **assurance of the quality and control of the bias within AI models themselves**. Given the impracticality of human-only audits in such an environment, employing **AI-Driven Audit**—that is, using AI to audit AI—will become imperative. Additionally, it will become essential to implement systems for **AI Model Auditing**, via a mechanism for auditing the AI auditors themselves. These form the foundation of the **AX (AGI Transformation)** concept presented in this book.

- **AI-Driven Audit (Audits Centered Around AI)**

  Full-Scope Auditing:

  Covers all critical risks and controls across every business process and every location comprehensively. Eliminating reliance on sampling significantly reduces the risk of fraud or misconduct occurring outside traditional audit scopes.

  Real-Time Auditing:

  Moves beyond periodic audit schedules (annual or quarterly) and implements continuous monitoring by AI. Each transaction is instantly screened for anomalies, generating immediate alerts. This approach enables swift reporting and response at the moment an issue emerges, dramatically limiting potential damage.

- **AI Model Auditing (Auditing the AI Auditors)**

  Regularly assesses algorithms and training data used by AI auditors. Checks objectively for indicators such as increasing false positives, maintenance of explainability, and any discriminatory elements within training datasets, thereby ensuring the reliability and credibility of the AI auditors themselves.

Through such **AI-Driven Audit**, incorporating both full-scope and real-time methods, combined with robust **AI Model Auditing**, organizations can effectively manage the explosive transaction speeds and the black-box nature expected in the 2030s, thus strengthening corporate governance.

(2) The Transformative Power of Full-Scope Auditing

At first glance, the concept of auditing everything comprehensively might seem impractical. However, creating a well-structured Process-Risk-Control (PRC) database and enabling AI auditors to leverage it can make this vision quite feasible.

A **PRC database** is a comprehensive inventory that lists all business processes and their associated risks and controls across every location. If organized properly—detailing control verification methods, thresholds, and integrated data sources for AI auditors—automatic verification by AI auditors becomes realistic. (See Chapter 6, "A Closer Look: Building the PRC Database as the Foundation for AI-Driven Audit," for detailed guidance.)

- **Liberation from Extensive Manual Verification:**

  AI auditors automatically perform verification tasks across all processes and locations based on the PRC database, eliminating exhaustive manual audit work traditionally performed by human auditors.

- **Freedom from Sampling Limitations:**

  AI auditors perform continuous, real-time monitoring of every transaction around the clock, 365 days a year. This eliminates reliance on sampling methods that can leave significant risks undetected.

- **Dramatic Improvement in Risk Detection:**

  Previously, limited audits sometimes missed fraudulent activities simply due to chance. A full-scope approach ensures that critical risks are detected systematically rather than left to luck.

As audit coverage expands and the early detection of fraud and misconduct improves, CEOs and boards of directors gain greater confidence in making bold business decisions. This positions audits as strategic enablers of proactive, growth-oriented management.

(3) Benefits of Real-Time Monitoring

Real-Time Monitoring involves immediate log analysis upon transaction execution, promptly issuing alerts when thresholds or abnormal patterns are detected. The benefits of this approach are evident:

- **Immediate Response to Limit Damage:**

  Errors or fraudulent activities in A2A transactions are identified instantly, enabling interventions before issues compound into extensive damage.

- **On-Demand Reporting to Management:**

  Instead of annual or quarterly reports, management is alerted immediately when substantial risks arise, facilitating rapid decision-making and responsive actions.

- **Improved Organizational Agility:**

  At an operational level, cooperation improves because personnel recognize that early consultations with auditors will lead to quicker resolutions. This transforms audits from periodic checks into an everyday governance, risk, and compliance (GRC) partnership.

Of course, managing alert frequency is critical to prevent operational teams from becoming overwhelmed, placing a premium on AI Auditor calibration and threshold-setting. With effective fine-tuning, real-time management of ultra-high-speed, high-volume transactions—previously impractical with sampling—becomes achievable, delivering auditing methods well-aligned with the business environment anticipated by 2030.

2.4 Shifting the Auditor's Role Toward Consulting

(1) The Era of AI-Driven Assurance Tasks

As AI assumes responsibility for routine assurance tasks such as evidence validation and anomaly detection, **human auditors can pivot towards consulting-oriented activities**, including business improvement proposals and strategic advising. This transformation from auditing as a post-facto check to **auditing as a consultative function supporting management** represents a major opportunity for auditors.

- **Reduction in Routine Tasks**

  Since traditional tasks such as interviewing and gathering audit documentation and data are handled by AI auditors, human auditors will be able to focus their efforts on evaluating the root causes and strategic implications of risks.

- **Support for Higher-Level Decision-Making**

  Leveraging risk insights identified by AI auditors, human auditors will gain bandwidth to engage proactively with management and operational teams, discussing acceptable risk levels and improvement initiatives, thereby delivering concrete consulting outcomes.

(2) Proactive Consulting by Human Auditors

Consider a scenario in which AGI autonomously manages financial processes and immediately sends alerts regarding any detected anomalies. Human auditors become critical in distinguishing between input errors, underlying business model flaws, and cyberattacks, and then proactively propose targeted improvement initiatives. Human auditors thus can actively provide consultative guidance in key areas, such as:

Operational Improvements

- **Inventory Management Optimization**

  Auditors analyze AI-generated logs and numerical data to identify excess inventory or waste. They diagnose underlying causes and recommend optimal inventory levels and streamlined processes.

- **Streamlined Procurement Processes for Improved Cash Flow**

  When AI detects procedural redundancies or repeated errors, auditors delve deeply into the root causes, prioritizing corrective measures and aligning implementation timelines with management.

- **Initiatives for Cost Reduction and Quality Improvement**
  Auditors utilize AI-provided data to support the review of processes and the adoption of new tools. They facilitate cross-functional improvements, enhance departmental collaboration, and assist in goal-setting.

New Business Risk Evaluation

- **Market Expansion Scenario Analysis**

  Using market intelligence compiled by AI auditors, human auditors conduct comprehensive risk assessments, evaluate ROI, and develop multiple business expansion scenarios, assisting executive-level decision-making.

- **Qualitative Evaluation of Regulatory and Financial Risks**

  Human auditors offer comprehensive evaluations of qualitative risks—including regulatory changes, political shifts, and social dynamics—and recommend specific risk mitigation strategies to management

- **Advisory and Alternative Solutions for Business Planning**

  Auditors provide insights into alternative strategies, such as targeting different market segments or revising partnership strategies, highlighting risks and opportunities that AI alone may overlook.

ESG and Sustainability Evaluations

- **Social Impact Evaluation of AI-Detected Risks**

  Auditors interpret AI-aggregated data from societal perspectives (e.g., CO_2 emissions, working conditions), delivering recommendations to the executive team regarding sustainability improvements.

- **Enhancing Governance Through Stakeholder Engagement**

  If AI identifies stakeholder concerns, auditors translate these findings to management and provide strategic advice to enhance transparency, stakeholder communication, and corporate governance.

As these examples illustrate, auditors will not only continue detecting and addressing fraud and errors, but will also evolve into strategic partners significantly contributing to corporate value enhancement. This shift represents the expected role of auditors from the 2030s onwards.

2.5 The Future Enabled by AX (AGI Transformation)

Through this chapter, you have gained a clear understanding of the transformative business environment anticipated by 2030—marked by explosive growth in A2A transactions, increasing AI complexity and opacity, and rapid international regulatory evolution. Collectively, these factors are poised to render traditional auditing methodologies obsolete. Practices such as Rotational and Limited-Scope Auditing and sampling-based testing risk becoming dangerously inadequate, leading inevitably to severe assurance gaps.

Conversely, by undertaking AX (AGI Transformation) initiatives and establishing a foundation of **Full-Scope Real-Time Auditing**, your organization will be able to:

- **Rapidly Detect Fraud and Misconduct:** Addressing issues within minutes rather than months, thereby significantly reducing potential financial and reputational damage.

- **Directly Manage Risks and Support Strategic Management:** With internal audit clearly visualizing risks, management can confidently pursue proactive investments and bold M&A strategies.

- **Pivot Toward Consulting-Focused Roles:** By entrusting routine audits to AI, human auditors can dedicate greater focus to value-added areas such as business performance improvement, ESG considerations, and strategic risk management.

In short, with 2030 rapidly approaching, the imperative and potential value of beginning your organization's AX journey has never been greater.

KEY TAKEAWAYS FROM THIS CHAPTER

1. **In 2030, AI-to-AI (A2A) transactions will fundamentally reshape business activities.**

   AI agents autonomously executing contracts and settlements without human intervention will lead to an explosive increase in trans-action volumes. This shift will significantly outpace decision-making cycles associated with traditional auditing methods.

2. **Traditional methods—such as Rotational and Limited-Scope Auditing and sampling-based testing—will no longer be adequate.**

   Legacy auditing practices involving sampling merely a handful of transactions from vast pools will dramatically increase the likelihood of overlooking significant risks and fraud.

3. **Transitioning to AI-driven, Full-Scope Real-Time Auditing is essential.** Implementing a system where **AI continuously monitors all locations and transactions 24/7, instantly detecting and flagging anomalies**, becomes critical. This will enable organizations to address risks promptly and proactively, minimizing potential damage.

4. **Addressing increasingly complex and opaque AI models is indispensable.**

As AI decision-making logic becomes more intricate and opaque—resulting in "black box" scenarios where humans cannot fully comprehend the rationale—regularly conducting **AI Model Auditing** and implementing **Explainable AI (XAI)** will become vital.

5. **Auditors' roles will evolve toward proactive consulting.**

With AI handling routine assurance tasks, human auditors can increasingly concentrate on value-added consulting activities, such as recommending business improvements and advising management strategically, evolving into indispensable **Trusted Advisors** who support executive leadership.

6. **The implementation of AX (AGI Transformation) will determine corporate futures.**

Companies adopting AX by 2030 will dramatically enhance their risk management capabilities and leverage proactive governance to gain competitive advantage. Conversely, firms neglecting to do so will face heightened risks of significant fraud and substantial losses.

LOOKING AHEAD TO THE NEXT CHAPTER: INTRODUCING THE AXCELERATION FRAMEWORK

This chapter clearly outlines that the year 2030 will represent a major turning point for internal auditing. We must fully acknowledge the reality that **traditional Rotational and Limited-Scope Auditing, along with sampling-based testing**, will become virtually obsolete in a world where A2A transactions are routine and AI autonomously makes critical business decisions. The shift to **Full-Scope Real-Time Auditing** is therefore inevitable and indispensable.

In subsequent chapters, I will delve into how exactly organizations can proceed with internal audit AX (AGI Transformation). Using the five key dimensions of MCOST (**Methodology, Culture, Organization, Skillset, Technology**) and navigating through the five stages of AEPIE (Assess → Envision → Pilot → Implement → Elevate), I aim to provide a clear roadmap for successfully implementing audit transformation.

Even if you feel "this is not yet relevant for my company" or "the implementation cost seems too high," remember that the year 2030 is not far away. The decisions and actions you take now will likely define your internal audit department's position and your organization's overall risk profile for the next

5–10 years. It is my hope that the AX framework introduced in this book will inspire you to move beyond outdated practices and embrace a new era of **proactive auditing tailored for the A2A and AGI era**.

Taking that first step opens a new world of possibilities. Whether you struggle to keep pace with A2A transactions or turn them into a source of innovation depends entirely on actions taken in the next few years. As you move to the next chapter and grasp the detailed workings of the **AXceleration Framework**, I encourage you to visualize what you can accomplish within your own organization and audit function. I believe it will serve as a critical guidepost on your transformative journey.

A CLOSER LOOK: WHAT IS CONSULTING IN INTERNAL AUDIT?

—Synergies Between Assurance and Advisory—

When hearing the term "internal audit," many typically imagine it to be a department whose main role is to point out fraud, errors, and control deficiencies—a purely "checking" function. However, in recent years, **consulting (advisory) activities within internal auditing** have been attracting significant attention. Consulting in internal audit refers to advisory services aimed at supporting the achievement of organizational objectives, playing a critical role in contributing to both the "defensive" and "proactive" sides of a business.

Differences Between Consulting and Assurance Activities

In internal auditing, **assurance activities** focus on providing independent and objective evaluations of the effectiveness of governance, risk management, and controls, thereby delivering confidence (assurance) to stakeholders. This is the traditional core function of internal auditing: assessing the design and operating effectiveness of controls and encouraging improvements when issues arise, representing the "defensive" aspect of auditing.

In practice, however, assurance and consulting are rarely clearly separated. Even within a single audit process, auditors might initially emphasize assurance when evaluating the effectiveness of controls, then shift to a consulting approach when recommending improvements after identifying deficiencies. Yet many audit departments today still devote the majority of their resources to assurance activities, leaving insufficient time for consulting services.

Increasing Consulting Opportunities in the Age of AGI

With the arrival of the era in which **Artificial General Intelligence (AGI)** deeply permeates corporate activities, routine and large-scale data checking and comprehensive monitoring can be entrusted to AI auditors. Consequently, human auditors will have more resources available to shift toward proactive consulting roles. As described in earlier chapters, adopting **AI-Driven Audit** will enable instant cross-checking of massive numbers of transactions and contracts, automatically detecting risks or fraud indicators. This will allow human auditors to focus more extensively on control evaluation and improvement recommendations.

Thus, internal auditing—which has traditionally primarily fulfilled a "checking" function—can evolve into a genuine partner role on which senior management relies to identify risks and opportunities. In the AGI era, internal auditors will have an unprecedented opportunity to actively support organizational growth and innovation.

Differences from Strategy and IT Consultants

Hearing the word "consulting," many people think of strategy consultants such as McKinsey or IT consultants such as Accenture. However, the consulting roles undertaken by internal audit departments differ somewhat in their approach.

- **Strategy Consultants**

  They primarily advise on top-level strategic decisions, such as "which markets the organization should enter."

- **IT Consultants**

  They generally focus on optimizing and implementing systems, such as "deploying ERP systems to streamline business processes."

In contrast, internal audit consultants concentrate on **Governance, Risk Management, and Compliance (GRC)**, advising executives and operational teams on issues like "how much risk should be accepted" or "to what extent control deficiencies must be addressed," based on the organization's risk appetite and the current business environment. A solid "defensive" foundation empowers organizations to boldly pursue proactive investments—including leveraging AI—and launching new ventures. This balance between risk and return is the distinctive strength of internal audit consulting.

Assurance and Consulting as "Two Wheels of the Same Vehicle"

Assurance provides businesses with objective confidence, while consulting propels business improvement and growth. These two functions are not in conflict; rather, they complement each other as "two wheels of the same vehicle." As the AGI era advances, and internal audit departments utilize AI to automate assurance tasks, human auditors can increasingly dedicate themselves to sophisticated consulting activities, thereby gaining recognition from management and stakeholders as a trusted advisor.

For instance, when internal auditors utilize vast amounts of data detected through continuous AI monitoring to propose specific process improvements, management can immediately make informed decisions. The deeper integration of AI and consulting positions internal auditors as indispensable key players simultaneously supporting the defensive and proactive facets of business.

Conclusion: In the AGI Era, Consulting Proficiencies Will Differentiate Internal Audit

With the advent of AGI, the "defensive" (assurance) aspect of auditing is likely to be significantly delegated to AI. This transition will enable human internal auditors to excel in consulting functions—proactively contributing to business improvements, risk response proposals, and strategic advice to senior management. Assurance and consulting are far from mutually exclusive; rather, they mutually enhance each other. Leveraging AI enables internal audit to shift toward higher-value-added activities.

In short, **AI-Driven Audit represents a substantial opportunity to elevate internal audit to the role of a right-hand partner to management.** How effectively internal audit departments can capitalize on this opportunity by 2030— to enhance organizational influence and contributions—will likely determine their ultimate success or failure.

Chapter 3
Overview of the AX Framework— AXceleration

—The Era of AGI Demands More Than Partial Implementation—

INTRODUCTION: WHY PARTIAL IMPLEMENTATION OF AI-DRIVEN AUDIT WILL BE INSUFFICIENT

In the preceding chapters, we examined the anticipated arrival around 2030 of an era characterized by ultra-high-speed AI-to-AI (A2A) transactions. We concluded that relying primarily on conventional methods such as Rotational and Limited-Scope Auditing and sample-based verification could lead to severe assurance shortfalls. As A2A transactions increasingly dominate operations, traditional human-led rotation audits, in which auditors periodically visit selected locations, will inevitably fall short in comprehensively covering organizational risks. Consequently, the risks of overlooking malfunctions or fraudulent activities within increasingly opaque, black-box AI systems will increase significantly.

On the other hand, successfully implementing **Full-Scope Real-Time Auditing** with AI auditors at its core could systematically uncover fraud and risk factors, thereby elevating corporate governance to unprecedented levels. Yet, realizing true **AI-Driven Audit** demands far more than simply adopting AI auditing tools. Partial or isolated implementation often results in operational failures or superficial usage, and organizations must instead pursue holistic transformation across multiple interconnected domains, including **Methodology, Culture, Organization, Skillset**, and **Technology** (MCOST).

In this chapter, we provide a comprehensive introduction to **AXceleration**, an AX framework designed specifically to facilitate this multi-dimensional reform in a structured manner. The defining feature of the AXceleration framework is that it clearly highlights the necessity of simultaneously upgrading all five MCOST elements and systematically breaks down this transformation process into five distinct steps: **Assess, Envision, Pilot, Implement, and Elevate (AEPIE)**. By doing so, it provides clear guidance on "when," "what areas," and "how" to implement change effectively.

3.1   What Is the AX Framework?

(1) Definition of AX (AGI Transformation)

AX (AGI Transformation) for internal auditing is a comprehensive concept designed to fundamentally transform internal audit practices to effectively respond to the dramatic changes brought about by the spread of **Artificial General Intelligence (AGI)** and the rapid expansion of **AI-to-AI (A2A)** transactions. Crucially, this is not merely about partially introducing AI, but about **placing AI at the very core of auditing operations** and achieving a genuine transformation.

- **Significance of positioning AI as Core, not merely Support:**

  In a post-2030 world, where **A2A** transactions and decision-making processes multiply and accelerate rapidly, traditional human-centric approaches such as **Rotational and Limited-Scope Auditing** and sample-based verification will inevitably reach their limits. Without embracing a **Full-Scope Real-Time Auditing** approach that continuously monitors all domains, organizations risk overlooking numerous frauds and control weaknesses. To effectively address this challenge, internal audits must be redesigned around AI-driven automated audits as their central operating principle.

- **Necessity of AI Model Auditing:**

  Implementing AI does not simply solve everything. Indeed, the increased reliance on AI also introduces the challenge of its algorithmic "black-box" nature. Thus, a critical aspect of the AX approach is establishing an effective **AI Model Auditing** mechanism to regularly evaluate the basis of AI decisions and monitor bias risks.

In other words, AX goes beyond marginal improvements to traditional audits, requiring transformative reforms at a much deeper level—including organizational culture and performance evaluation systems.

(2) Five Key Transformation Domains (MCOST) in the AGI Era

The AX framework breaks down transformation efforts into five domains referred to as MCOST. This categorization arose from the author's practical experience, highlighting the essential requirement of a holistic approach—encompassing culture, talent, organizational structure, and more—for effective implementation of AI-Driven Audit. The MCOST domains are the following:

1. Methodology

- **Shift to Full-Scope Real-Time Auditing**

  Move away from conventional **Rotational and Limited-Scope Auditing** by leveraging technologies like a comprehensive Process-Risk-Control (PRC) database. Utilize AI to enable extensive and continuous audit coverage.

- **Reengineering Audit Processes for AI-Driven Audit**

  Overhaul existing audit processes entirely, aligning them with new requirements such as AI Model Auditing and advanced data analytics methods, thereby ensuring higher quality and efficiency.

2. Culture

- **Overcoming Resistance to AI Adoption**

  Address misconceptions like "AI will take away our jobs" or "audits are restrictive," fostering instead a positive, AI-friendly Culture that encourages collaboration between humans and AI.

- **Fostering a Culture Accepting of Proactive Auditing**

  Promote organizational recognition of internal auditing as an entity contributing positively to corporate value creation. Implement comprehensive change management to nurture a spirit of bold, fearless innovation.

- **Strong Commitment from Senior Leadership**

  Leadership from top management is crucial in driving organizational cultural transformation. Leaders must clearly articulate vision and policy to align the entire organization.

3. Organization

- **Establishing a Project Management Office (PMO)**

  Create a centralized body to oversee comprehensive auditing transformations and large-scale projects, clearly delineating roles and responsibilities to facilitate smooth organizational restructuring

- **Forming AI Audit Teams and Consulting Enhancement Teams**

  Assemble specialized talent skilled in AI implementation and staff with strong consulting proflciencies to deliver new forms of value.

- **Global Integration and Restructuring Reporting Lines**

  Revise reporting structures and enhance coordination with global offices to ensure rapid and standardized information sharing and optimal information flow.

4. Skillset

- **Clarifying Skills via Skill Mapping**

  Develop a clear skill map of auditors' competencies, identify gaps against required skills for AGI-era auditors, and highlight areas requiring reskilling.

- **Strengthening Auditor Skills for the AGI Era**

  Reinforce skills across critical areas: AI competencies (AI literacy, data analytics), Consulting proficiencies (consulting mindset, business acumen), GRC expertise (governance, risk management, compliance, internal controls), and Global adaptability (cross-cultural skills, language proficiency, regulatory awareness).

- **Training and Certification Systems**

  Develop internal and external training programs and support professional certifications to elevate overall organizational skill levels.

5. Technology

- **Introducing AI Auditors (Axel)**

  Develop and deploy an AI-driven system capable of autonomously performing verification tasks and real-time monitoring of transactions to detect risks.

- **Establishing AI Model Auditing**

  Implement robust AI Model Auditing mechanisms to systematically evaluate AI auditors for accuracy and bias, maintaining the reliability of AI-Driven Audit.

- **Ensuring Compliance with Security and Privacy Regulations**

  Actively manage information leakage and privacy risks associated with AI usage, integrating closely with Business Continuity Planning (BCP).

The interconnection of these five MCOST elements constitutes both the complexity and the rewarding challenge of the AX transformation. Implementing only one or two elements in isolation will not suffice; simultaneous progress across these interconnected domains is necessary to realize the full potential and impact of AX.

(3) Five Steps to Effectively Drive AX Implementation (AEPIE)

To ensure the success of large-scale internal auditing reforms through AX, we recommend a structured five-step process: Assess → Envision → Pilot → Implement → Elevate (AEPIE). Based on the author's extensive practical experience, this method takes into account stakeholder psychology, changes in their mindsets, and investment decision timelines:

1. Assess (Current-State Evaluation)

- **Requirements Definition & Fit-Gap Analysis**

  Conduct thorough assessments of existing auditing methodologies, organizational structures, staff skillsets, and technological environments. Quantify and visualize the gaps between current states and desired future states. Clarify prioritized areas for immediate intervention while fostering urgency and understanding among management and the board.

2. Envision (Vision Setting)

- **Developing Plans & Securing Top-Level Agreement**

  Develop a clear roadmap for achieving **Full-Scope Real-Time Auditing**, detailing when and how specific locations and processes will adopt AX, along with estimated investments and ROI. Gain consensus and secure resources from senior management.

3. Pilot (Pilot Implementation)

- Testing and Demonstrating Quick Wins

  Pilot AX initiatives in select locations or processes, achieving quick, tangible results to reduce organizational resistance. Quickly identify and address implementation issues and communicate early successes broadly, laying foundations for company-wide rollout.

4. Implement (Full-Scale Implementation)

- **Organization-wide Deployment & Cultural Integration**

  Roll out AI-Driven Audit across all organizational and global domains, firmly embedding **Full-Scope Real-Time Auditing** as standard practice. Concurrently undertake organizational restructuring (such as forming AI Audit Teams and Consulting Enhancement Teams), while revising appraisal systems to embed proactive auditing into organizational culture.

5. Elevate (Continuous Improvement)

- **Ongoing Upgrades & Enhanced Value**

  Continuously upgrade AI Model Auditing capabilities and further strengthen consulting functionalities, regularly evolving audit practices. Integrate new technological advancements to further reduce risks and proactively support new business and innovation initiatives.

Adopting this AEPIE framework will help translate general AI implementation plans into tangible phases, clearly highlighting "what to do now" and "what comes next."

It is crucial to understand that these steps are not strictly linear but iterative and agile—often executed in parallel (e.g., Assess and Envision, Implement and Elevate). Organizations are encouraged to flexibly customize this process to align with their unique circumstances.

3.2 What is the AXceleration Matrix (MCOST × AEPIE)?

(1) Structure of the AXceleration Matrix

To systematically organize the overall picture of the AX framework, the **AXceleration Matrix** is particularly useful. This matrix combines the five elements of MCOST (**Methodology, Culture, Organization, Skillset, and Technology**) with the five steps of AEPIE (**Assess, Envision, Pilot, Implement, and Elevate**).

- The matrix consists of **25 intersections (e.g., Methodology × Assess, Methodology × Envision, etc.)**, enabling you to clearly outline the specific initiatives required at each point.

- For instance, at the intersection of **Methodology × Assess (M×A)**, you might define tasks such as:

  Measure current audit coverage rates and dependence on sampling to quantitatively identify assurance gaps.

- Similarly, at **Technology × Pilot (T×P)**, you could include actions like:

  Pilot the AI Audit Platform in selected areas and verify alert accuracy.

Using this matrix allows you to visualize who addresses which issues, at which stage, and involving which stakeholders, effectively preventing omissions or duplications.

(2) Practical Examples of Using the Matrix

The following are some practical examples demonstrating how specific tasks can be outlined clearly within the AXceleration Matrix:

Methodology × Envision (M×E)

- Define Key Performance Indicators (KPIs) for Full-Scope Real-Time Auditing (coverage rate, reporting frequency, etc.) and incorporate these into the AX transformation plan.

- Draft a roadmap for AI-Driven Audit (e.g., Year 1: Main domestic sites, Year 2: Overseas branches).

Culture × Pilot (C×P)

- Conduct briefings and small-scale achievement presentations during the pilot phase for auditors and audited departments concerned about AI-Driven Audit.

- Proactively communicate success stories via internal SNS or company newsletters to alleviate resistance and facilitate effective change management.

Skillset × Implement (S×I)

- Deploy AI-literacy training company-wide, providing essential knowledge not only to auditors but also to key members in audited departments.

- Expand consulting proficiencies and business analysis training to all team members, standardizing improvement proposals leveraging risk insights from AI-Driven Audit.

Technology × Elevate (T×E)

- Enhance capabilities of the AI Audit Platform by incorporating Explainable AI, zero-trust security, and cloud failover configurations.

- Continuously evaluate next-generation architectures in alignment with AGI advancements, ensuring ongoing adaptability of Full-Scope Real-Time Auditing to the company's growth pace.

Such clearly defined initiatives will help teams understand precisely what tasks are executed at each phase, and what outcomes they aim to achieve.

(3) AXceleration: An Approach to Rapid Transformation

The reason for coining the term **AXceleration** (a combination of **AX (AGI Transformation)** and **Acceleration**) is to vividly illustrate the concept of rapidly accelerating transformation through AX implementation.

Concurrent Updates Across All Dimensions

- If **Methodology** moves ahead but **Culture** remains resistant, the implementation will stall. Similarly, changes in **Organization** without parallel advances in **Technology** will lead to superficial and ineffective results.

- Therefore, it is essential to simultaneously advance **all MCOST dimensions** within the AEPIE framework to achieve significant, short-term successes.

Speed and Vision for the Future

- From 2030 onward, the era of **AGI and A2A** is expected to bring about unprecedented business transformation speed.

- Although incremental progress ("small steps") is valuable, a certain degree of boldness and accelerated actions are crucial for keeping pace with competitors and rapidly evolving market conditions.

By populating each of the 25 intersections within the AXceleration Matrix with concrete initiatives, even complex, large-scale projects become clearer and more manageable. This clarity provides distinct definitions of **tasks and performance indicators for each phase,** facilitating better organizational engagement and smoother execution.

KEY TAKEAWAYS FROM THIS CHAPTER

1. **Comprehensive Reform Is Essential for Internal Audit Transformation (AX) in the AGI Era**

   From 2030 onward, as Artificial General Intelligence (AGI) and AI-to-AI (A2A) transactions become mainstream, traditional audit approaches such as Rotational and Limited-Scope Auditing and sampling-based testing methods will reach their limits. Hence, a fundamental shift toward Full-Scope Real-Time Auditing is essential.

2. **Simultaneous Transformation Across MCOST (Methodology, Culture, Organization, Skillset, Technology)**

   Simply introducing AI tools will not be enough to achieve successful AI-Driven Audit. It is crucial to simultaneously and interactively transform all five interconnected domains—audit methodology, corporate culture, organizational structure, personnel skillsets, and technology infrastructure.

3. **Gradual Implementation Through AEPIE (Assess → Envision → Pilot → Implement → Elevate)**

   Large-scale transformations like AX require a phased approach. Resistance can be reduced and overall success rates increased by starting with **Assess** (current state evaluation), clearly articulating a vision (**Envision**), conducting small-scale pilot projects (**Pilot**) to build successful cases, moving on to organization-wide implementation (**Implement**), and finally, carrying out continuous improvement (**Elevate**).

4. **Visualizing Reform with the AXceleration Matrix (MCOST × AEPIE)**

   Utilizing the AXceleration Matrix, which intersects the five MCOST elements with the five AEPIE steps, clearly illustrates **when, in what area,** and **how** transformations should occur. This provides a structured approach to centralized project management, promoting efficient and swift reform implementation.

5. **Partial Adoption Is Insufficient for the A2A Era**

   Before the rapid expansion of AGI and A2A in the 2030s, organizations must fully embrace **Full-Scope Real-Time Auditing**, placing AI at the core of audit processes. Failing to do so risks significant assurance gaps, with increased likelihood of overlooking fraud and critical business risks.

LOOKING AHEAD TO THE NEXT CHAPTER: IN-DEPTH EXPLORATION OF AX STEPS

This chapter introduced the AX framework, emphasizing the five key MCOST elements and five AEPIE steps, managed comprehensively through the AXceleration Matrix. This framework serves as a roadmap for organizations facing the A2A transaction era and considering how to evolve their internal audit function.

However, practical questions remain unanswered, such as:

- "What exactly should we assess in the current state evaluation (Assess)?"
- "How do we quantify the gaps and formulate KPIs?"
- "What steps are required when envisioning the roadmap for Full-Scope Real-Time Auditing (Envision)?"
- "What specific processes are necessary during pilot implementation (Pilot)?"

To address these concrete questions, the next chapters will delve deeper into each AEPIE step in detail.

By understanding how to approach each MCOST element at every AEPIE stage, the AX framework evolves from a theoretical concept into an actionable roadmap. This transforms it from abstract ideals into a practical tool that clarifies precisely **what needs to be done now.**

In the upcoming chapter on "**Assess** (Current State Evaluation)," we will thoroughly explore how to identify and visualize the current state of your audit methodology, culture, organization, skillsets, and technology. Clearly recognizing the extent to which your organization's AI adoption may be lagging is the critical first step toward successful AX implementation.

Chapter 4
Assess—Evaluating Current Capabilities and Identifying Fit & Gap

—Shining a Light on Hidden Risks and Untapped Potential—

INTRODUCTION: THE FIRST STEP OF AX IS UNDERSTANDING YOUR CURRENT STATE

In previous chapters, we have discussed the dramatic impacts that Artificial General Intelligence (AGI) will have on corporate activities and the emerging new roles for internal audit within that landscape. At the core of this book is the concept of **AX (AGI Transformation)**, advocating for the establishment of **Full-Scope Real-Time Auditing**, where AI is not just supplementary but central to auditing functions.

However, attempting to realize this vision within your organization without precisely understanding your current audit capabilities and gaps could lead to costly backtracking, excessive spending, and delays. Hence, the initial step, **Assessing the Current State**, is critically important. Insights gained in this stage will lay a robust foundation for the roadmap to be developed in the next chapter (**Envision**) and will help secure internal support and commitment. Without a thorough initial assessment, there is a significant risk of confusion at implementation or loss of executive buy-in. Therefore, a detailed, multi-faceted assessment is indispensable.

In this chapter, we will apply the five MCOST elements (Methodology, Culture, Organization, Skillset, Technology), introduced previously, to systematically evaluate the gap between your existing internal audit framework and the ideal auditing model needed for the AGI era. This Fit & Gap analysis clearly highlights company-specific issues, forming the basis for roadmap creation (**Envision**) in subsequent chapters.

4.1 Assessing Methodology: Evaluating Current Audit Practices and Identifying Gaps

4.1.1 Revisiting the Concept of Full-Scope Real-Time Auditing

Let's first reconfirm the meaning of **Full-Scope Real-Time Auditing**. With the rapid advancement of AGI and generative AI, a world of instantaneous and massive-scale AI-to-AI (A2A) transactions and decision-making is imminent. Under these conditions, traditional methods such as **Rotational and Limited-Scope Auditing** or partial sampling-based testing will clearly become insufficient due to their inability to keep up with transaction scale and speed.

Therefore, the central feature of the new auditing methodology for the AGI era is leveraging AI to monitor all locations, all processes, and all risks, detecting anomalies immediately at the point of transaction, and issuing real-time alerts. Of course, there might be a substantial gap between this ideal vision and your current reality. It is crucial to numerically evaluate your current audit coverage—determining how many locations and risks your audit actually encompasses, and whether your real-time audits are truly immediate or lagging behind, conducted annually or even less frequently. Clearly quantifying these points makes the improvement opportunities highly visible.

4.1.2 Measuring the Gap with Current Human-Driven Audit

(1) Quantifying Audit Coverage (Location and Process)

To realize Full-Scope Real-Time Auditing, it's highly effective to quantify limitations in your current audit coverage. Let's measure coverage rates through two key approaches:

Location-Based Coverage

- Suppose your group has 100 global locations; determine how many locations are actually audited annually.

- Besides the simple number of locations, consider additional metrics such as coverage based on sales ratio or profit contribution.

- Revealing a statistic like "only 10% of locations are included in annual audit plans" can strongly communicate urgency to top management.

Process, Risk, and Control (PRC) Coverage

- Develop a comprehensive inventory of core business processes, risks, and associated controls at each location (the PRC database), then quantify how thoroughly they are currently audited.

- For example, if a particular site's purchasing process has ten key risks with five controls each (50 controls total), yet you currently only test 25 controls, your control-based coverage at that site is 50%.

- Clearly documenting this combined location-and-control-based coverage at a global scale vividly illustrates the gap between your current state and the necessary full-scope, all-processes ideal for the AGI era.

(2) Dependence on Sampling-based Testing

Next, analyze your current reliance on sampling-based testing. If your auditing methods are primarily based on statistically extracting dozens to hundreds of samples for manual review, the emergence of millions of A2A transactions could sharply increase risks of undetected fraud or critical issues that remain hidden outside your sampled data. Evaluate:

- How many samples you test annually versus the size of the entire transaction population.

- Historical cases of fraud or irregularities that occurred outside your samples.

- Variability of sampling standards across locations or departments.

For many organizations, sampling remains a necessity due to resource constraints. It is crucial at this stage to clearly communicate the limitation of sampling as a ticking time bomb in the AGI era.

(3) Audit Rotation Frequency & Distance from Real-Time

Another frequently overlooked issue is your audit cycle. Traditionally, audits in many organizations occur at significant intervals, such as once every three to five years for major locations or quarterly and annual reports. In an A2A-driven world, lengthy audit intervals can allow fraud or anomalies to escalate rapidly.

- Is your audit planning strictly annualized and inflexible?
- How frequently do you conduct audits? Do you report findings immediately, or is there a lag of months?
- Is there a culture or protocol for real-time alerts or spontaneous reporting of anomalies?

Assessing these points clarifies how far your current structure is from genuine real-time auditing capabilities.

4.1.3 Learning from Historical Fraud and Incidents

Another valuable angle of methodology evaluation is revisiting historical fraud, scandals, or significant incidents. Key questions include: Why didn't our current audits catch this issue? Did this occur due to rotation gaps? Was this issue outside sampled items?

- Fraud occurred entirely outside your audit scope, delaying detection.
- Incidents were within your scope but not caught due to limited sampling
- International locations had insufficient local regulatory understanding
- Limited IT literacy restricted comprehensive data verification.

Identifying these lessons clarifies risks that will exponentially escalate in the AGI era, vividly illustrating the urgency of implementing Full-Scope Real-Time Auditing.

4.1.4 Evaluating Global Audit Methodology Standardization

Lastly, do not overlook the importance of assessing global audit methodology standardization. In multinational organizations, audit approaches often vary by region or subsidiary, potentially creating critical gaps. In preparation for AGI-driven auditing, having a uniform global methodology is essential.

- Do individual locations have separate internal audit departments using different audit standards and methods?
- Is there a centralized plan from headquarters to unify audit methodologies globally, or are local factors causing barriers?

- Identify obstacles, including cultural resistance, language barriers, or differences in IT infrastructure.

In the AGI era, AI-Driven Audit achieves far greater effectiveness if approached uniformly across the organization. Identifying these potential barriers at the Assess stage helps proactively manage challenges in subsequent implementation phases.

4.2 Assessing Culture: Evaluating Current Organizational Culture and AI Readiness

4.2.1 Top Management Commitment and Organizational Culture

Strong support from top management is essential for successful AX implementation. This support is especially critical in multinational companies, where differences in perspectives and interests between headquarters and field operations are common. Initial resistance and budget allocation challenges will be influenced significantly by the extent to which the CEO and the board communicate that **AI-Driven Audit is essential to the company's transformation**.

Assess the following points:

- **How proactive is the CEO, CFO, or Audit Committee in supporting the introduction of AI-Driven Audit?**

- **Has the management clearly established a budgetary policy to facilitate AX implementation?**

- **Is there an existing track record of top management leading other DX (digital transformation) projects directly?**

If top management holds skeptical views, such as "**AI-Driven Audit? AI can't be trusted; our current audit approach is sufficient**," the AX promotion team must clearly present past fraud incidents, current audit coverage metrics, and other persuasive data to foster a shared sense of urgency. Conversely, strong top management backing can ease implementation by overcoming resistance at the operational level from a top-down approach.

4.2.2 Psychological Resistance to AI: Conservatism in the Internal Audit Department and Change Management

Internal audit departments, traditionally responsible for preventing fraud and managing corporate governance, tend to adopt a conservative stance. Introducing AI could raise several points of resistance or concern:

- **"Will AI take over auditors' jobs?"**

- **"Who will bear responsibility for accuracy and false alerts? Will numerous false positives by AI disrupt operations or confuse auditors?"**

- **"We lack the capacity or bandwidth to learn new AI-related skills and knowledge."**

Leaving these psychological barriers unaddressed could seriously hinder effective AX implementation. During the **Assess** phase, it is essential to gather frank opinions from auditors through surveys and small group meetings, categorizing stakeholders into **Resisters**, **Neutral Parties**, and **Early Adopters**. This segmentation helps clarify how to tailor messages for each group when developing the subsequent change-management plan. For example, leveraging success stories from pilot projects can effectively persuade resisters.

4.2.3 Cooperation of Audited Departments and Organization-wide DX Promotion Culture

Even if the internal audit department is fully committed, smooth progress of AX depends substantially on the cooperation of audited departments. If audited departments perceive the introduction of AI-Driven Audit negatively—as an increase in their burden (**"They'll demand more data than ever"** or **"Additional controls will complicate our processes"**)—the project could stall.

Evaluate the following:

- **How cooperative are audited departments currently, and have there been notable conflicts or issues during past audits?**

- **Is there an established culture of embracing company-wide DX and IT projects, or is there deep-rooted resistance and stubbornness in maintaining existing processes?**

- **Do audited departments view internal auditing as merely compliance checks, offering limited tangible value?**

If significant resistance exists, develop a clear communication strategy that highlights benefits, such as **"early detection of expense fraud or inventory loss, leading to more efficient budget management."** Additionally, cooperating with departments already advancing DX initiatives to achieve **small successes** during the Pilot phase can help showcase AX's practical benefits and ease resistance.

4.3 Assessing Organization: Evaluating Current Audit Structure and Resource Allocation

4.3.1 Internal Audit Organizational Structure and Resources

In this book, we emphasize the ideal scenario for AGI-era audits as establishing dedicated **AI Audit Teams** and **Consulting Enhancement Teams**. Therefore, during the Assess stage, it is vital first to clearly understand your current internal audit organization's structure and available resources.

Assess these points:

- **How is the internal audit department currently structured at headquarters (e.g., operational audit teams, IT audit teams, global audit teams, planning teams)?**

- **Do global branches maintain their own local audit teams? If so, what is their size and role distribution?**

- **How many auditors currently possess deep expertise in data analytics or AI development?**

Understanding these details will help determine whether your organization needs external recruitment or if existing members can be upskilled to form future AI Audit Teams and Consulting Enhancement Teams.

4.3.2 Balance Between Assurance and Consulting Activities

A common issue among audit departments is the predominance of assurance work and a limited engagement in consulting activities. According to the **"2025 North American Pulse of Internal Audit,"** conducted by the IIA in 2025, **"many Chief Audit Executives (CAEs) wish to increase consulting services, but approximately 75% of internal audit work currently focuses on assurance, leaving only**

about 25% for consulting." This imbalance occurs because auditors spend significant time on verification tasks and routine documentation, leaving little time for proactive advisory roles.

However, AX implementation will facilitate **Full-Scope Real-Time Auditing**, reducing auditors' burdens related to verification and documentation and enabling a greater focus on consulting—such as improvement proposals and strategic business advice.

During the Assess phase, evaluate the following:

- **What percentage of internal audit department activities currently consists of consulting work?**

- **How frequently have audited departments proactively requested advice on operational improvements or risk management from internal auditors?**

- **How significant are current resource and skill shortages (including mindset) for performing consulting engagements effectively?**

Clarifying these issues allows for a concrete projection such as "**If AI implementation significantly streamlines assurance activities, we can increase our consulting work share to X%.**" This specific vision can be strongly persuasive for senior management.

4.3.3 Visibility of Audit Workloads and ROI (Return on Investment)

When promoting AX, top management will naturally be concerned about cost-effectiveness. Therefore, clearly visualizing current audit workloads and annual costs during the Assess phase helps lay the groundwork for estimating cost reduction effects from AI automation later on.

Consider these points:

- **Estimate the labor costs, travel expenses, and external consultant fees incurred for each audit.**

- **Calculate the annual total audit costs and compare them against the audit coverage rate.**

- Apply hypothetical scenarios such as "**Introducing AI-Driven Audit could potentially reduce audit workloads or improve productivity by XX%, reallocating resources to consulting activities.**"

Having this information prepared allows you to concretely illustrate ROI to executives during the subsequent Envision phase, facilitating the development of a persuasive "**AX Implementation Plan**."

4.4 Assessing Skillset: Evaluating Current Auditor Skills and Competencies

4.4.1 Establishing a Skill Map

In the AGI era, internal auditors will require a significantly broader range of skills and knowledge than previously necessary. Specifically, auditors must acquire expertise in AI competencies, Consulting proficiencies, Governance, Risk, and Compliance (GRC), internal control knowledge, and Global adaptability. Many auditors likely already possess foundational knowledge in GRC and internal controls. However, domains such as AI competencies, Consulting proficiencies, and Global adaptability are often insufficiently developed among auditors.

Therefore, it is crucial to create a **comprehensive Skill Map** that clearly illustrates the current skill levels of all members within the audit department compared to those required for the AGI era. In the Assess phase, consider evaluating the following competencies in detail:

- **AI competencies:**
  - o Basic proficiency in programming languages such as Python
  - o Understanding of machine learning models and hands-on experience with data analytics tools
  - o Familiarity with auditing methodologies utilizing AI-driven tools

- **Consulting proficiencies:**
  - o Problem-solving frameworks and effective presentation skills
  - o Skills for negotiation and communication with senior management and clients
  - o Ability to propose solutions for new business development and operational improvements

- **Global adaptability:**
  o Multilingual communication skills

  o Cross-cultural understanding and experience auditing overseas subsidiaries

  o Fundamental knowledge of international standards and foreign regulations

- **Areas of Expertise and Years of Experience:**
  o Individual expertise fields (e.g., IT, finance and accounting, manufacturing processes)

  o Participation in cross-functional projects

  o Track record in leadership and management roles

Clearly outlining such a Skill Map facilitates the creation of concrete action plans for recruitment or external consultant support during subsequent Pilot and Implement stages.

4.4.2 Essential Skill for the AGI Era (1): AI Competencies

Of particular importance in the AGI era are the AI-related skills required to collaborate effectively with AI audit systems. Auditors must position themselves as **skilled AI users**, capable of accurately interpreting AI-generated anomaly detection results and conducting thorough AI Model Auditing.

Key skills include:

- **AI Literacy:** Fundamental knowledge of machine learning, deep learning, and anomaly detection algorithms

- **IT Skills:** Operational proficiency with BI tools, basic programming, and SQL queries

- **Data Analysis Skills:** Expertise in statistical methods and visualization techniques necessary for analyzing extensive transaction data

Collaborative work with AI dramatically improves outcomes when auditors deeply understand **how AI derives its decisions**. Assessing the current level of such skills within your department is crucial. Establishing plans to enhance these skills, if insufficiently developed, will be pivotal to successful AX implementation.

Moreover, AI competencies require ongoing updates to keep pace with rapid technological advancements. Auditors hesitant about acquiring these competencies risk being left behind in the AGI era.

4.4.3 Essential Skill for the AGI Era (2): Consulting Proficiencies

In the AGI era, human auditors will increasingly focus on high-value consulting activities. With AI handling routine assurance tasks, auditors should shift their energies towards providing proactive operational improvements and strategic advisory aligned with management's risk appetite.

Key consulting competencies include:

- **Consulting Mindset:** Moving beyond mere **identification of deficiencies** towards proposing actionable improvements that tangibly benefit the organization
- **Business Acumen:** Ability to provide realistic and value-added advice by understanding overall organizational performance, financial indicators, and external business environments
- **Alignment with Risk Appetite:** Given rapid environmental changes, auditors must understand management's risk tolerance to determine appropriate advisory levels

In the Assess phase, evaluating the current auditors' consulting experience and management perspective is vital. Significant gaps identified at this stage indicate the necessity for targeted training programs or engaging external consulting expertise.

4.4.4 Essential Skill for the AGI Era (3): GRC and Internal Control Expertise

While AI effectively handles assurance tasks, human auditors retain ultimate responsibility for reviewing audit outcomes and driving necessary improvements. Without deep knowledge in Governance, Risk, Compliance (GRC), and internal controls, auditors may struggle to interpret and act upon AI-generated findings adequately.

Critical competencies in this domain include:

- **GRC Expertise:** Understanding governance frameworks, risk assessment methods, compliance requirements, and fraud prevention practices

- **Internal Control Expertise:** Ability to interpret AI-detected control deficiencies, identify root causes accurately, and provide effective guidance for improvement

Far from diminishing, auditors' specialized knowledge will become even more valuable as AGI technology evolves. Auditors must competently guide AI systems, correct false positives, and mitigate inherent biases. Thus, during the Assess phase, it is necessary to carefully identify the level of GRC expertise within the audit team and prepare targeted enhancement strategies.

4.4.5 Essential Skill for the AGI Era (4): Global Adaptability

Implementing **Full-Scope Real-Time Auditing** globally necessitates seamless communication across international subsidiaries. Essential to this is auditors' global adaptability.

Key aspects include:

- **Language Proficiency:** Despite increasing reliance on AI translation, auditors still require basic skills in reading and writing documents and emails effectively

- **Cross-Cultural Competence and Local Regulation Knowledge:** Auditors must thoroughly understand diverse legal frameworks, business customs, and communication styles across different countries to avoid misunderstandings or conflicts during audits

- **Routine Collaboration with Overseas Offices:** Smoothly exchanging information via online meetings or chats and effectively utilizing AI audit tools as a common communication platform

In particular, cross-cultural communication skills are critical to gaining acceptance for improvement proposals at local subsidiaries. Assessing **how extensively language and cultural differences affect global auditing activities and how the audit department currently addresses them** will identify crucial development areas. Although AI supports translation, nuanced interpretation remains a distinctly human role.

4.5 Assessing Technology: Evaluating Current Technological Infrastructure and Capabilities

4.5.1 Status and User Satisfaction of Existing GRC and Audit Tools

To introduce AI-Driven Audit effectively, understanding the current adoption and utilization of existing GRC and auditing tools is essential. Many companies face common challenges: partial use of available GRC or risk management tools, failure to leverage their full functionalities, or reverting to Excel due to cumbersome user interfaces.

Evaluate the following in the Assess phase:

- **Current usage of GRC tools, including utilized features (e.g., alert management, document management)**
- **Level of satisfaction among audit staff and audited departments with existing tools**
- **Potential compatibility or expandability of existing tools to incorporate AI auditing capabilities, or necessity for complete system replacement**

Detailed assessments in this area will enable concrete strategic decisions—such as **retaining and enhancing existing tools** versus **introducing new systems**—in the subsequent Envision phase.

4.5.2 Status of Company-wide Data Platforms and System Integration

Achieving **Full-Scope Real-Time Auditing** requires robust infrastructures capable of aggregating real-time or periodic data from all global subsidiaries, enabling AI auditors to perform effective monitoring. However, multinational or large enterprises often encounter significant challenges, such as inconsistent data formats across subsidiaries or legacy systems lacking modern API integration capabilities.

Assess the following areas:

- **List of ERP, accounting, inventory management, and purchasing systems used across all subsidiaries**
- **Status of API integrations, ETL processes, and data lakehouse arrangements**
- **Existing internal plans for system integration or collaboration with ongoing DX initiatives**

Inadequate integration at the system level risks severely limiting AI audit platforms due to inaccessible or fragmented data. Identifying these barriers clearly during the Assess phase helps estimate the scope and scale of necessary investments early in the project.

4.5.3 Environment and Constraints on Utilizing Generative AI (LLM)

Many companies currently experiment with Large Language Models (LLM), such as ChatGPT. However, using generative AI seriously in auditing contexts introduces heightened confidentiality and privacy challenges. Carefully evaluate these points during the Assess phase:

- **Current internal use of generative AI (e.g., proprietary in-house platforms or public cloud solutions)**
- **Existence of clearly defined AI usage policies established by compliance or legal departments**
- **Availability of secure mechanisms for safely entering sensitive audit information into generative AI tools or significant restrictions on data input due to confidentiality concerns**

If stringent security policies prohibit using cloud-based generative AI solutions, it may become necessary to establish on-premises or private cloud-based LLM environments. Early identification of these constraints will ensure better-informed planning of future AI Audit Platform architectures.

KEY TAKEAWAYS FROM THIS CHAPTER

1. **The First Step of AX Is a Multifaceted, Quantitative "Assessment"**

   Introducing Full-Scope Real-Time Auditing to meet the demands of the AGI era requires accurately understanding your organization's current audit system across five dimensions (Methodology, Culture, Organization, Skillset, and Technology), clearly quantifying gaps, and obtaining a perspective of the deficit relative to the ideal state.

2. **Methodology: Clearly Identify the Limits of Audit Coverage and Sampling Dependency**

   Quantitatively demonstrate the current audit coverage rate of locations and business processes, dependency on sampling methods, and the audit rotation cycle. **By clearly highlighting the limitations of traditional auditing methods in coping with the ultra-high-speed,**

high-volume transactions of the AGI era, you can effectively raise awareness among senior management.

3. **Culture: Uncover Top Management Commitment and Internal Resistance**

   Evaluate senior executives' commitment to AI implementation, as well as psychological resistance within both audit departments and audited divisions. **Establishing the groundwork for a Change Management strategy that leverages quick wins from Pilot implementations is crucial at this stage.**

4. **Organization: Clarify the Current Audit Structure and Consulting Work Ratio**

   Clearly assess the existing audit team structures, resource allocation, and the proportion of assurance versus consulting activities. **This provides foundational data to demonstrate the potential for improved operational efficiency and enhanced value creation through AX implementation.**

5. **Skillset: Use a Skill Map to Visualize Gaps in AI Competencies + Consulting Proficiencies**

   Identify and visualize current skill levels within your audit department, including **AI literacy, data analytics skills, consulting abilities, and global adaptability**, to clarify training and recruitment needs for auditors to thrive in the AGI era.

6. **Technology: Evaluate Existing Audit Tools, Data Infrastructure, and AI-Related Constraints**

   Evaluate user satisfaction and expandability of existing GRC and audit tools, examine company-wide system integration status, and identify constraints related to security and privacy in Generative AI usage. **This evaluation helps set the stage for necessary system upgrades or new implementations required for successful AX implementation.**

LOOKING AHEAD TO THE NEXT CHAPTER: FROM "ASSESS" TO "ENVISION"

In this chapter, we have thoroughly explored the importance of a detailed, multi-dimensional assessment before fully launching the AX initiative. **By clearly visualizing the gap between the ideal audit state (Full-Scope Real-Time Auditing) and the current audit approaches (Rotational and Limited-Scope**

Auditing, sampling-based testing), you effectively convey to stakeholders the urgency for transformation and the necessity of investment.

The findings from this Assess phase are critical for creating an actionable AX plan and roadmap in the next chapter ("**Envision**"). Specifically, these findings will be utilized as follows:

- **Demonstrate to senior management:**

  "Our current audit covers only 10% of locations; there's an X% risk of undetected issues lying beyond sampled areas."

- **Propose the need for a global standardization of audit methodology:**

  "Since audit methodologies at overseas locations are inconsistent, we must first establish unified global standards."

- **Clarify the need for reskilling and training programs:**

  "Our organization lacks sufficient personnel with AI literacy; therefore, we must conduct X training sessions over the next year."

- **Include data integration strategies in the AX roadmap:**

  "Due to inconsistent data infrastructure across subsidiaries, we must implement API integration in clearly defined phases to ensure the success of Pilot initiatives."

The Assess phase uncovers real-world challenges and builds awareness that is critical for successful AX implementation. Thorough assessment at this stage minimizes potential issues in later Change Management and Pilot stages, forming a solid foundation to secure support from senior management and audited departments.

Moving forward, in the next chapter, we will discuss precisely how to overcome identified challenges and gaps and concretely design internal audits for the AGI era. Specifically, we will explore how to articulate your AX vision and secure top management's buy-in. You will learn how to engage your entire organization, turning the concept of **Full-Scope Real-Time Auditing** from abstract vision into tangible reality.

Let's delve into practical strategies and proven know-how for making this transformation successful.

Chapter 5

Envision—Strategizing the AX Framework for AI-Driven Audit

—Designing a Bold Roadmap from Insight to Impact—

INTRODUCTION: CHARTING THE NORTH STAR FOR AX (AGI TRANSFORMATION)

In Chapter 4, "**Assess (Current State Evaluation)**," we undertook a comprehensive analysis of your current internal audit landscape, clearly identifying the Fit & Gap against the essential components for the Artificial General Intelligence (AGI) era. Now, we move forward into the "**Envision (Vision Formulation)**" stage, designing how internal audit can fully integrate AI as its core.

As AGI advances, and transactions or decisions increasingly become AI-to-AI (A2A)—high-speed, large-scale interactions between AI systems—the traditional approaches such as **Rotational and Limited-Scope Auditing** and sampling-based testing will inevitably fall short. Conversely, transitioning to **Full-Scope Real-Time Auditing** presents an unprecedented opportunity to proactively manage risks and accelerate strategic management.

However, simply advocating for a new auditing vision may be mere wishful thinking, in the absence of clearly defined Return on Investment (ROI), alignment with corporate strategy, and concrete implementation roadmaps. Without these elements, it will be challenging to secure commitment from the CEO or the Board. Thus, this chapter explains how to close the gaps identified previously across each dimension of MCOST (**Methodology, Culture, Organization, Skillset, Technology**), formulate a clear vision, establish a concrete roadmap, and obtain executive buy-in.

The Envision phase is crucial for AX success because the **AX Implementation Plan** developed here becomes the North Star for the subsequent stages— **Pilot (Initial Implementation)** and **Implement (Full-scale Implementation)**. To smoothly drive significant company-wide transformations, it's essential to clearly articulate objectives, execution steps, timelines for ROI realization, and ultimately gain agreement from both senior management and the broader organization.

5.1 Envisioning Methodology: Defining the Vision for AI-Driven Audit

5.1.1 Aligning Audit Methodology with Corporate Strategy and Risk Appetite

To fundamentally transform auditing methods for the AGI era, it is critical to align your audit methodology with corporate strategy and risk appetite. This involves not merely expanding the scope of auditing but clarifying how much risk your organization is willing to accept (**Risk Appetite**) and communicating clearly to management the tangible benefits of implementing **Full-Scope Real-Time Auditing**.

For example, a corporation aggressively expanding into emerging markets faces increased political and compliance risks. Implementing AI-driven real-time detection would significantly enhance their ability to manage such risks proactively. Conversely, organizations emphasizing cost reduction can utilize real-time AI monitoring across the supply chain to swiftly identify waste or fraud, achieving substantial cost improvements. Clearly linking auditing strategy to corporate objectives strengthens the case for AX implementation, positioning auditing as an enabler of strategic acceleration.

5.1.2 Implementing Full-Scope Real-Time Auditing

The cornerstone of methodological innovation lies in transitioning to **Full-Scope Real-Time Auditing**. Historically, auditing methods selectively examined specific locations or processes, often relying on manual checks and sampling techniques. However, the rapid proliferation of AI-to-AI transactions (A2A) in the AGI era necessitates a comprehensive shift:

- **Full-Scope Auditing**:

  Covers all critical risks and controls across every location and process, eliminating reliance on sampling. This will significantly reduce risks related to fraud and misconduct beyond traditional audit boundaries.

- **Real-Time Auditing**:

  Rather than scheduled audits (annual or quarterly), AI will continuously monitor transactions, instantly detecting anomalies and alerting stakeholders, significantly minimizing potential damages by enabling rapid response.

Given practical considerations of risk and cost, it's advisable to adopt a phased approach: initially testing AI-Driven Audit within key processes (e.g., procurement, accounting), demonstrating success, and progressively scaling to additional processes and international locations. Clearly outline this phased approach within the AX plan at the Envision stage.

5.1.3 Setting KPIs and Roadmaps to Avoid Unrealistic Goals

While **Full-Scope Real-Time Auditing** is conceptually appealing, executives will naturally question its feasibility. To address skepticism, set clear KPIs and detailed timelines indicating milestone achievements:

- **Audit Coverage Rate**:

  Quantify current coverage by location and control points. Set specific targets such as coverage rates of X% after one year, increasing to Y% within three years.

- **Reporting Lead Time**:

  Demonstrate how real-time auditing significantly shortens reporting cycles (e.g., reducing from months-long audits to days or weeks).

- **Cost and Labor Efficiency**:

  Showcase efficiency gains through automation of assurance tasks, reallocating auditor resources toward higher-value consulting tasks, clearly articulating the expected ROI.

Defining clear KPIs across specific periods (Year 1, Year 2–3) and creating a detailed roadmap of feature implementation help persuade management and operational units about the plausibility and practicality of your plan, facilitating budgetary and resource support.

5.2 Envisioning Culture: Fostering a Collaborative AI-Friendly Culture

Significant hurdles to AI-Driven Audit often arise from organizational culture and psychological resistance. Leveraging issues identified during the Assess phase, clearly formulate strategies for cultivating an **AI-friendly Culture** where humans and AI collaborate harmoniously.

5.2.1 Transitioning to an AI–Human Collaborative Culture

In the previous assessment, various attitudes toward AI (resistance, indifference, or support) were identified. During the Envision stage, develop concrete steps to alleviate resistance and include them in your AX Implementation Plan:

- **Stakeholder Analysis**:

  Categorize key groups (top management, internal auditors, audited departments) into "supporters," "resisters," and "neutral," clearly summarizing their proportions and sentiments.

- **Action Plan Development**:

  Identify specific actions (top-down messaging, regular project updates, AI literacy programs, HR policy integration) for each stakeholder group, systematically reducing resistance through structured engagement.

- **Quantified Goals**:

  Set measurable KPIs, such as "within one year, over half the audit department views AI positively," or "within three years, at least 80% of audited departments recognize benefits of AI-Driven Audit."

Cultural change is gradual, necessitating clearly defined milestones within your roadmap, consistently monitored and adjusted over time. Detailed planning at the Envision stage significantly simplifies managing resistance during subsequent Pilot and Implement phases.

5.2.2 Regular Culture Surveys for Monitoring Progress

Periodic cultural surveys objectively measure cultural transformation, quantifying reductions in resistance and improvements in attitudes toward AI collaboration, thus becoming a critical indicator of project progress:

- **Pilot Stage Surveys:**

  Initially focus on internal audit teams, assessing anxieties, expectations, and workloads to validate effectiveness of quick wins in reducing resistance.

- **Implement Stage Surveys:**

  Expand surveys to the entire organization, including audited departments, measuring satisfaction with AI-Driven Audit, perceived benefits, and senior management's evaluation, tracking results as KPIs (e.g., "Cultural Maturity Index").

Regularly reporting survey outcomes enables continual refinement of your Change Management strategy, solidifying cultural changes over the long term.

5.2.3 The Importance of Tone at the Top

Strong, explicit commitment from top management—known as **Tone at the Top**—is crucial for effective cultural transformation. AX can be positioned as a critical corporate initiative by clear declarations from the CEO, board, and audit committee that "auditing must evolve with the AGI era" and "promoting human−AI collaboration in auditing":

- Clearly summarize the AX plan during the Envision phase, securing firm approval from senior management.

- Highlight both urgency (increasing A2A transactions, rising risk exposure) and opportunities (enhanced assurance via real-time auditing, expanded consulting functions), securing strong consensus.

- Regularly disseminate top-level messages encouraging early Pilot successes to motivate organization-wide adoption.

When executives visibly prioritize audit transformation, internal stakeholders recognize auditing reform as a strategic imperative, significantly easing operational resistance. Without strong top-level endorsement, AX risks becoming superficial, underscoring the importance of securing executive commitment during this crucial Envision stage.

5.3 Envisioning Organization: Structuring for AI-Enhanced Audit and Strategic Consulting

5.3.1 Team Structure: Establishing AI Audit Teams and Consulting Enhancement Teams

In the Envision phase, it is essential to clearly articulate the envisioned structure of the internal audit organization post-AX implementation. Central to this vision are two specialized teams: **AI Audit Teams** and **Consulting Enhancement Teams**.

- **AI Audit Teams**

  These teams are experts in operating AI models, managing data, and tuning anomaly detection algorithms. They handle routine assurance tasks by utilizing AI to process massive data volumes in real-time, significantly reducing manual workloads and allowing human auditors to focus on higher-value activities.

- **Consulting Enhancement Teams**

  Utilizing risk and internal control issues identified by AI, these teams focus primarily on providing consulting services. Beyond pointing out deficiencies, they proactively advise audited departments and management, contributing strategically to business improvements and value creation.

The timing for talent reinforcement and organizational restructuring can be clarified by presenting this organizational blueprint in the AX Implementation Plan along with a phased roadmap—such as initiating a small-scale AI Audit Team during the Pilot phase and formally launching Consulting Enhancement Teams during the Implement phase.

5.3.2 Re-envisioning Global Audit Team Structure

Multinational companies often have decentralized audit structures where headquarters and international subsidiaries operate independently with localized audit methodologies. However, achieving effective AI-Driven Audit requires a unified, standardized approach, enabling rapid and consistent global adaptability to AI-generated alerts. Key considerations include:

- Establishing priority handling for alerts (e.g., high-risk alerts immediately reported to headquarters, lower-risk ones handled locally).

- Identifying and addressing barriers to standardizing international audit methodologies (cultural differences, local regulations, IT infrastructure challenges).

- Sharing best practices and expertise from headquarters' AI Audit Teams with global subsidiaries through regular meetings and online collaboration platforms.

Mapping out this global restructuring vision during the Envision phase and incorporating initial pilot tests in select subsidiaries will streamline full-scale global rollout during the Implement phase.

5.3.3 Securing Budgets for AX Implementation

AX initiatives require significant investment in technology, tools, and talent development. Clearly articulating the expected Return on Investment (ROI) is critical to obtaining executive buy-in. ROI can be classified into two categories:

- **Defensive ROI**: Avoiding financial losses through early fraud detection, reducing regulatory compliance risks, enhancing corporate reputation, and significantly reducing audit hours through automation.

- **Offensive ROI**: Increasing the proportion of consulting activities within internal audit, leading to cost reductions, revenue growth through improved business advice, and strategic support for new business ventures.

A major objective of the Envision phase is presenting clear, compelling evidence—such as "AI-Driven Audit could avoid annual losses of $XX million" or "Consulting services will expand by XX%, leading to substantial cost savings."

5.4 Envisioning Skillset: Developing Next-Generation Auditors for the AGI Era

Internal auditors in the AGI era must possess a significantly broader skill set, including AI competencies, Consulting proficiencies, GRC (Governance, Risk, Compliance) knowledge, and Global adaptability. Drawing on gaps identified during the Assess phase, it is important to clearly map out the skills auditors must acquire, specifying targets for timing and the number of personnel involved.

5.4.1 Defining an Ideal Skill Map

In the Assess phase, we identified key skills needed for the AGI era. Examples include:

- **AI competencies** (AI literacy, data analytics, machine learning fundamentals)

- **Consulting proficiencies** (logical thinking, negotiation, business acumen)

- **GRC expertise** (governance, risk management, compliance, internal controls)
- **Global adaptability** (languages, local regulations, cross-cultural understanding)

Envisioning specifically how many auditors should acquire these skills by particular deadlines allows clear KPI definition, facilitating effective monitoring post-launch. For example, these could be formulated as "All auditors to complete basic AI literacy training in Year 1," "Consulting skills training plus overseas rotations in Year 2," and "Training XX senior auditors in advanced GRC expertise by Year 3."

5.4.2 Boosting Auditor Motivation and Engagement

While the AGI era requires significant auditor reskilling, some staff may view this as a source of uncertainty or an additional burden. Thus, initiatives to enhance learning motivation and positive messaging are essential, for example:

- Communicating how AI handling routine tasks will enable auditors to concentrate on consulting and advanced decision-making, broadening their career potential.

- Highlighting opportunities for career advancement within global subsidiaries or strategic planning departments upon acquiring new skills.

- Positioning skilled auditors as strong candidates for future leadership roles.

Consistent promotion of these positive visions by senior management and audit leaders, coupled with initiatives such as including training hours as part of working hours, will foster proactive engagement in learning.

5.4.3 Recruiting Talent from Inside and Outside the Organization

When certain skills cannot be fully addressed by reskilling alone, recruiting external specialists or internal transfers may be necessary. Potential scenarios include:

- **AI Experts**: Hiring external talent proficient in machine learning and data analytics to lead AI Audit Teams.

- **Consulting Professionals**: Recruiting former management consultants to strengthen Consulting Enhancement Teams

- **Internal Mobility**: Encouraging motivated personnel from other departments (IT, corporate planning, etc.) to join AX projects.

Based on talent gaps identified in the Assess phase, the Envision phase should clearly specify recruitment timing and job requirements. To ensure smooth project startup, it is advisable to initiate recruitment early—with a lead time of at least six months.

5.4.4 Planning Short-term and Long-term Reskilling and Recruitment

Differentiating between skills achievable through short-term training and those requiring longer-term cultivation helps establish realistic reskilling strategies. For instance:

- **Short-term AI competencies**: Basic machine learning principles, API integration, and AI ethics training can be completed within weeks to months.

- **Long-term AI competencies**: Developing specialists capable of advanced data analytics requires continuous practical experience and learning.

Similar distinctions apply to consulting proficiencies, GRC expertise, and global adaptability. Outlining these clearly in the AX Implementation Plan during the Envision phase, including annual target numbers and training budgets, enables streamlined reskilling execution during Pilot and Implement phases upon budget approval.

5.5 Envisioning Technology: Designing the AI-Driven Audit Platform

Finally, it is crucial to clearly envision technology infrastructure for AX implementation. Based on challenges identified during the Assess phase regarding legacy environments and data integration, this section specifies system requirements and investment plans to realize AGI-era auditing.

5.5.1 Defining AI Audit Platform Requirements and IT Investment Plans

Operationalizing AI-Driven Audit necessitates detailed platform requirement definitions and IT investment plans during the Envision phase, considering:

- **System Architecture**

  o Deciding between on-premises, cloud, or hybrid configurations.

  o Designing APIs to collect data from ERP or accounting systems across locations.

  o Implementing standardized external integration using Model Context Protocol (MCP) for AI Auditor and other tools.

  o Managing audit logs and models effectively, potentially via data lakehouse solutions.

- **Requirement Specifications**

  o Developing algorithms and prompts for automated verification.

  o Establishing either frequent batch or real-time streaming monitoring.

  o Managing workflow for alerts (priority setting, escalation rules).

  o Implementing robust **AI Model Auditing** (bias checking, audit log retention, explainability).

IT Investment Scale

  o Calculating required investments yearly, including integration costs with legacy systems and additional overseas requirements.

  o Outlining vendor selection and high-level implementation timelines.

  o Clearly defined plans in Envision enable smooth initial deployments during the Pilot phase.

5.5.2 Data Integration and Coordination

Implementing **Full-Scope Real-Time Auditing** involves addressing significant data integration challenges, especially when various locations use disparate ERP or legacy systems. Key strategies include:

- **API Integration Plans**: Determining data acquisition frequency and methods using REST APIs or ETL tools.

- **Short- and Medium-term Approaches**: Integrating primary procurement and accounting systems initially during the Pilot phase and expanding progressively

- **Data Cleansing and Mapping**: Standardizing inconsistent data across locations to facilitate effective AI processing.

Including these strategies in the Envision plan ensures clear direction and practical testing of data integration during Pilot phases.

5.5.3 Addressing Security, Privacy, and Regulatory Compliance

Given the immense real-time data processing inherent in AI-Driven Audit, integrating Security by Design principles from the outset is critical:

- **Zero Trust Models**: Regular validation of users and devices, adaptable for expanding A2A transactions.

- **International Regulatory Compliance**: Ensuring compliance with GDPR, EU AI Act, and state-specific U.S. AI regulations.

- **Business Continuity Planning (BCP)**: Outlining continuity measures should the AI Audit Platform encounter disruptions.

Documenting these considerations in the AX Implementation Plan, including required IT investments, talent allocation, and vendor engagements, ensures robust security planning for the Pilot and Implement phases.

KEY TAKEAWAYS FROM THIS CHAPTER

1. **The Envision Phase: Your North Star for Successful AX Implementation**

   For AX to be successful, internal audit transformation must clearly align with your company's business strategy and risk appetite, securing organization-wide consensus. Clearly defining ROI and developing a specific roadmap will significantly enhance the commitment from the CEO and board of directors.

2. **Methodology: A Step-by-Step Roadmap for Full-Scope Real-Time Auditing**

   While the ultimate goal is achieving comprehensive, real-time auditing across all locations and processes (**Full-Scope Real-Time Auditing**), it is unrealistic to roll this out across the entire organization simultaneously. Start by piloting AI-Driven Audit in influential areas (such as procurement or finance). Accumulate smaller successes first, then expand systematically.

3. **Culture: Strategically Transitioning to an AI-Friendly Culture**

    Clearly identify psychological barriers and organizational resistance. Develop a structured change management plan grounded in strong top-level commitment (**Tone at the Top**). Regularly conduct culture surveys to monitor progress and systematically reduce resistance in phases.

4. **Organization: Realigning Teams into AI Audit Teams and Consulting Enhancement Teams**

    Clearly design organizational structures that maximize automated assurance tasks using AI and high-value consulting activities performed by humans. Additionally, draft a roadmap for global standardization and reorganization of audit practices to leverage efficiencies internationally.

5. **Skillset: Strategically Developing Auditors' Essential AGI-Era Skills**

    Develop detailed reskilling plans specifying timeframes in which auditors must acquire key capabilities such as AI competency, Consulting proficiency, GRC expertise, and Global adaptability. Separate short-term training from longer-term skill-building strategies, and consider internal and external recruitment options to close skill gaps efficiently.

6. **Technology: Clearly Defining AI Audit Platform Requirements and Investment Plans**

    Articulate detailed system requirements for your AI Audit Platform, including architecture, data integration approaches, and security and privacy considerations. Create a comprehensive IT investment plan for both short-term and long-term phases, enhancing feasibility for successful Pilot and Implement phases.

LOOKING AHEAD TO THE NEXT CHAPTER: PILOT IMPLEMENTATION—TURNING VISION INTO TANGIBLE RESULTS

In this chapter, we have detailed the steps involved in the **Envision** phase— crafting an actionable AX Implementation Plan and roadmap based on gaps identified during the **Assess** phase and securing buy-in from executive management and relevant departments. By clearly outlining your vision for **Full-Scope Real-Time Auditing**, specifying change management approaches, skill development initiatives, and IT investment plans, you position your organization to minimize resistance and effectively drive transformation.

However, even the best-designed plans will leave lingering doubts. Prior to tangible evidence, people will always wonder if something is really achievable. Therefore, the next critical step is the **Pilot phase**. During this stage, selected locations or processes will run a limited-scope trial of AI-Driven Audit, aiming to quickly generate concrete short-term successes ("quick wins"). Demonstrating tangible results reduces organizational resistance and strengthens the case for broader investment.

In the following chapter, we will delve into how to effectively execute the **Pilot phase**. You'll learn how to strategically begin with impactful yet manageable areas—such as procurement or accounting—to demonstrate early success, shift departmental mindsets, and win executive confidence. This groundwork becomes crucial as you progress toward full-scale **Implementation**. We'll also explore the practical steps involved, anticipate common challenges, and underscore why successful pilot implementation is often the determining factor for the overall success of your AX initiative.

Chapter 6
Pilot—Achieving Quick Wins through Initial AX Deployment

—Proving the Power of AI Audit One Use Case at a Time—

INTRODUCTION: THE FIRST STEP TO LAUNCHING AI-DRIVEN AUDIT

In the previous chapter, **Envision**, we solidified our vision and roadmap for audit transformation in the era of **Artificial General Intelligence (AGI)**. Yet, no matter how excellent the plan, genuine organizational change won't happen unless it is practically tested and its benefits demonstrated clearly. This makes the **Pilot** phase absolutely critical.

The essence of the Pilot is to deliberately **avoid an all-at-once approach**, instead implementing **AI-Driven Audit** within a limited scope—specific processes or business areas—to achieve quick wins in a short timeframe. This method allows the organization to replace internal skepticism ("Does this really work?") with clear success stories, cultivating an attitude of curiosity and enthusiasm ("Can we have this in our department too?").

This chapter describes how to effectively proceed with the Pilot across the MCOST dimensions (Methodology, Culture, Organization, Skillset, and Technology). Introducing AI-Driven Audit in a small, defined scope serves as an invaluable "testing ground," providing insights from both successes and failures to inform the subsequent, broader **Implementation** stage. Thoughtful design of your Pilot is therefore essential, ultimately determining the success of the overall **AX (AGI Transformation)** effort.

6.1 Pilot Methodology: Testing AI-Driven Audit on a Limited Scale

6.1.1 Begin with Developing the PRC Database

To ensure successful Pilot implementation, start by building a robust **PRC (Process, Risk, and Control) database**, even within a limited scope. Without clearly structured PRC data, AI-Driven Audit cannot correctly identify which risks and controls to monitor, potentially leading to frequent false alerts or overlooked issues.

- **Narrow Your Scope Initially**

  Choose processes with high transaction volumes, significant risk exposure, and relatively organized data, such as procurement or accounting, to ensure quick and meaningful wins.

- **Systematize PRC Data**

  Take procurement as an example: document the workflow clearly ("vendor registration → ordering → delivery → inspection → payment") alongside associated risks (fictitious orders, excess inventory, price manipulation) and list related controls.

- **Convert Data into AI-Compatible Formats**

  Transition from paper-based checklists to digital formats, clearly specifying "Process/Risk/Control/Data Source/Threshold/Priority," laying the foundation for continuous AI monitoring.

By establishing this foundational PRC database within a limited domain, you create a reliable baseline. Achieving tangible results during the Pilot clarifies the pathway for future expansion to a broader, company-wide Implementation.

(*Note: For additional details, refer to the A Closer Look on the "PRC database" provided at the end of this chapter.*)

6.1.2 Pilot Transition: From Limited-Scope to Full-Scope Auditing

Pilot implementations typically begin with focused trials, such as at one location or within a single process. A full-company rollout from the start would drastically escalate costs and risks, so conducting small-scale experiments first and then sharing successes with leadership is ideal:

- Pilot full-scope audits in one region or a single process (e.g., North American branch, procurement process)

- Continuously monitor and document outcomes.

- Share pilot findings with executive management, emphasizing reduced risk and enhanced detection capabilities.

- Develop cost–benefit projections for scaling up across departments or global locations.

Through phased trials like these, you can dismantle perceptions that full-scope auditing is "unachievable," motivating stakeholders toward broader adoption.

6.1.3 Pilot Transition: From Sampling to Comprehensive Auditing

Traditional human-driven sampling will become untenable in the AGI era, characterized by vast numbers of **AI-to-AI (A2A)** transactions. Piloting comprehensive auditing for selected processes highlights the distinct advantages offered by AI:

- **Pilot Comprehensive Auditing**

  Have AI systems continuously inspect all procurement transactions, immediately flagging anomalies.

- **Identify Previously Undetected Risks**

  Uncovering hidden anomalies or fraudulent activities previously missed by sampling clearly showcases the unique value of AI-Driven Audit.

  However, excessive AI-generated alerts can overwhelm the operational team. Establish careful alert thresholds and priority settings (high-risk alerts trigger immediate reports, lower-risk issues compile weekly) to demonstrate the tangible value of AI-generated alerts.

6.1.4 Pilot Transition: From Periodic Rotational to Real-Time Auditing

The ultimate objective is to conduct auditing in real-time—detecting risks as transactions occur. Initially, Pilot implementations can compare real-time auditing alongside traditional periodic audits to quantify the improvement in detection speed:

- Deploy real-time auditing systems to instantly alert the audit team of suspicious transactions.

- Quantify improvements by directly comparing detection speeds against conventional rotational audits.

- Clearly demonstrate real-time advantages to executives to simplify future investment decisions for full-scale deployment.

Successfully showcasing the benefits of real-time auditing during the Pilot will significantly reduce obstacles to future organization-wide Implementation.

6.2 Pilot Culture: Building Initial AI Acceptance Within the Internal Audit Team

One of the earliest barriers to **AX** implementation is often psychological resistance within the internal audit department. Conservative organizational cultures may fuel fears like "Will AI take our jobs?" or aversion to large-scale process changes. It is crucial to address this resistance by demonstrating early successes during Pilot implementation.

6.2.1 Top Priority for Initial Adoption: Reducing Resistance Within the Internal Audit Department

Internal auditors often experience substantial initial anxiety and resistance toward AI-Driven Audit. Typical concerns include fear of job displacement ("Will AI take my job?") and accountability issues ("Who takes responsibility for AI-generated false alarms?"). Successfully overcoming these anxieties hinges on early, tangible achievements.

- **Clearly Present Quick Wins**

  Demonstrate concrete results of AI-Driven Audit early in the pilot— such as identifying multiple cases of potential fraud within the first week. For instance, clearly communicating that "AI-Driven Audit detected 10 suspicious transactions indicative of fictitious billing within seven days" significantly boosts credibility.

- **Highlight Reduced Workload and Increased Value for Auditors**

  Clearly communicate how automating routine checks via AI frees auditors to concentrate on high-value tasks like consulting and deeper risk analysis, thereby enhancing job quality and visibility within the organization.

- **Encourage Auditors to Experience AI Benefits First-Hand**

  Actively involve internal auditors in processing AI-generated alerts. Let them directly observe workload reductions and fewer overlooked risks, creating genuine, positive experiences that effectively dispel resistance.

6.2.2 Targeted Approaches for Different Stakeholder Segments

Within the audit department, attitudes toward AI typically range from enthusiastic supporters to anxious skeptics and indifferent staff. Acknowledge these variations and develop targeted approaches:

- **Enthusiastic Advocates (Pro-AI)**

  Involve them centrally in Pilot implementations. Have them publicly communicate positive results, leveraging their credibility to mitigate skepticism within the broader team.

- **Indifferent Group (Neither Enthusiastic Nor Resistant)**

  Clearly illustrate personal and direct advantages, such as "AI adoption can reduce overtime" or "significantly fewer data entry errors," helping them recognize practical benefits and promoting buy-in.

- **Resistant Group (Strongly Skeptical or Fearful)**

  Provide individualized communication, thoroughly explaining that AI is merely a supportive tool and that final decisions remain human-controlled. Emphasize opportunities for auditors to enhance their career through consulting-focused tasks as routine auditing activities diminish.

Widely communicating Pilot successes through internal channels (e.g., intranet, departmental meetings) gradually shifts the departmental sentiment toward accepting AI-Driven Audit as beneficial. This foundational shift significantly smooths the pathway to broader implementation.

6.3 Pilot Organization: Launching a Small-Scale AX Initiative

When initiating the Pilot, determining the organizational structure is crucial. Rather than undertaking major organizational reform at one stroke, it's typical to first launch a small-scale AX pilot project managed by a Project Management Office (PMO). The insights gained here significantly accelerate the broader implementation phase.

6.3.1 Establishing the AX Pilot Project

To formally kick off an AX pilot project, the following steps are effective:

Selection of Project Leaders and Members

- Recruit motivated volunteers from internal audit staff, particularly those in areas most suitable for pilots, such as North American procurement or accounting, and IT department engineers.
- Select leaders who are enthusiastic about AI-Driven Audit, knowledgeable in the domain, and capable of effective internal coordination.

Clarify Pilot Goals and Objectives

- Clearly set quantifiable and qualitative goals such as: "Within three months, activate AI-Driven Audit in the procurement process and detect at least XX suspicious transactions early," or "Reduce audit reporting lead times from annually to monthly."
- Utilize a clear **Work Breakdown Structure (WBS)** and set key milestones and schedules, transparently illustrating the project's value to the broader organization.

Emphasize Execution with a Small, Agile Team

- Smaller teams typically move faster and make quicker decisions. Fewer, highly skilled members help accelerate improvement cycles.
- After the Pilot concludes, share outcomes organization-wide, setting the stage for expanded implementation.

Clearly articulating the project's objectives and visualizing schedules and tasks through a WBS helps all members align towards the same goals, maximizing efficiency.

6.3.2 The Necessity of a Project Management Office (PMO)

As AX adoption progresses, diverse departments—including IT, Human Resources, and international offices—become involved. Establishing a PMO during the Pilot phase can provide the following benefits:

Unified Management of Issues and Progress

- Centralize information in the PMO to quickly identify, visualize, and prioritize issues, avoiding fragmented information management.

Efficient Resource Allocation

- The PMO centrally manages limited personnel and budgets, strategically focusing resources to resolve bottlenecks quickly.

Leveraging Successes and Lessons Learned

- Document successes and failures from the Pilot clearly, creating reusable knowledge for future deployments across other locations and processes in the broader implementation.

Even at the Pilot stage, running a compact PMO is crucial for systematically gathering insights, significantly benefiting subsequent company-wide rollouts.

6.3.3 Early Involvement of International Offices

In global enterprises, delaying involvement of international offices often leads to unexpected obstacles in later Pilot stages due to local regulations, languages, and cultural differences, potentially causing significant delays. Thus, it's beneficial to share Pilot information early with key international stakeholders, occasionally including overseas offices in initial small-scale trials.

Regular Information Sharing via Online Meetings

- Routinely update overseas audit leaders on Pilot progress and issues, collecting their feedback and suggestions.

Early Identification of Local Regulations and Cultural Factors

- Identify critical factors early, such as compliance with the EU AI Act or the need for multi-language dashboards.

Include International Offices in the Pilot Scope

- When possible, add at least one overseas location to the Pilot project, laying groundwork for smoother global expansion.

These strategies help ensure smoother global deployment during the Implement phase.

6.4 Pilot Skillset: Enhancing Auditor Skills Through Targeted Training and OJT

Entering Pilot implementation without sufficient AI competencies or consulting proficiency can significantly diminish the benefits of AI tools. Thus, it is essential to provide intensive training and on-the-job training (OJT) to Pilot members, enabling them to confidently master required skills.

6.4.1 The Importance of In-person Training and OJT for Pilot Members

Pilot success depends significantly on team skill improvement and motivation. Since Pilot members will become AX pioneers, providing direct, interactive in-person training and practical OJT is particularly valuable:

Effectiveness of In-person Training

- Online training alone limits real-time understanding checks and engagement.

- In-person interactions allow immediate feedback, quick resolution of questions or concerns, and foster team cohesion and shared purpose.

Practical Skill Development Through OJT

- Members directly apply AI operation and consulting proficiency acquired during training within real Pilot scenarios.

- Actively involve motivated younger auditors alongside experienced personnel, enhancing their practical skills through direct experience.

- Plan proactively to cultivate members who will form the core of future AGI-era audit teams.

Fostering AI Literacy and Confidence Through Training

Essential AI fundamentals and practical operational knowledge must be understood clearly, reducing anxiety and promoting effective utilization:

- **Basic AI knowledge:**
  o Machine learning and deep learning fundamentals
  o Understanding false positives/negatives
  o AI bias and privacy protection issues

- **Operational Know-How:**
  o Appropriate responses and escalation flows when AI generates alerts
  o Prioritization and review processes for alerts

- **Direct Link Between Training and Operations:**

  o Set immediate practical application schedules, ensuring skills are solidified quickly through direct experience.

Strengthening Consulting Skills and Mindset

AI handling routine auditing tasks allows human auditors to engage more in high-value consulting:

- **Consulting Fundamentals Training:**

  o Logical thinking, problem-solving methods, and process improvement strategies

  o Methods to transform risks or audit findings into concrete business improvements

Fostering a Proactive Audit Mindset:

  o Emphasize proactive improvement suggestions and value creation, not just risk reporting.

Sharing Success Stories and Building Knowledge:

  o Document successful Pilot cases, such as clear cost reductions or business improvements, further motivating team members.

6.4.2 Refining Training Content Based on Feedback

Pilot-phase training functions as a prototype for eventual organization-wide rollout. Actively soliciting and utilizing Pilot member feedback helps continually enhance training effectiveness:

- Conduct post-training surveys and discussions to identify unclear points or desired deeper content.

- Continuously test training formats (in-person, online, hybrid) and materials (videos, workshops), aiming for optimal learning experiences.

Ideally, training programs will be significantly refined during Pilot implementation, enhancing their effectiveness during the larger-scale Implement phase.

6.5 Pilot Technology: Validating the AI Audit Platform Within a Controlled Scope

The main objective of the Technology Pilot phase is to get the **AI Audit Platform** prototype operational, even at a small scale. Based on system requirements defined in Assess and Envision phases, determine precisely what will be prototyped and which areas will be continuously monitored.

6.5.1 Building a Prototype of the AI Auditor with Agile Development

To achieve AI-Driven Audit during Pilot, develop a functioning prototype of the **AI Audit Platform** based on previously defined requirements. Prioritize agile methodologies rather than waterfall approaches:

- **Prioritize Essential Features First:**

  Quickly develop crucial functions such as anomaly detection and alert notification. Immediately test these operationally, allowing rapid iteration based on real-world feedback.

- **Focus on Iteration:**

  AI technology evolves rapidly; agile methods enable more responsive adjustments and easy incorporation of new requirements.

- **Parallel Development and Training:**

  Concurrently overhaul audit methods and train personnel. Delaying these tasks until after AI tool development risks significant implementation delays.

Commercial AI auditing systems may not yet exist, necessitating custom development or external vendor collaboration. The critical mindset is to rapidly develop a minimum viable product (MVP) and continuously improve through practical operations.

6.5.2 Security Considerations During the Pilot Phase

Since Pilot implementation remains limited, extensive security infrastructure is typically deferred to the Implement phase. Nevertheless, initial minimum standards for access control and data protection are essential for safely conducting Pilot activities.

Detailed implementations of zero-trust models and specific international regulatory compliance are planned comprehensively during full-scale Implementation, ensuring robust security when rolling out globally.

KEY TAKEAWAYS FROM THIS CHAPTER

1. **The Pilot Phase: The Critical Turning Point for AX Success**

   The **Pilot phase** is pivotal to the success of the entire **AX (AGI Transformation)** project. Conducting a small-scale trial of **AI-Driven Audit** within specific, limited processes or domains—and demonstrating concrete results (**quick wins**)—will significantly influence the success of future company-wide expansion. Achieving clear, measurable Pilot successes makes the next implementation phase smoother and more credible.

2. **Methodology: Trialing Full-Scope Real-Time Auditing on a Limited Scale**

   Deploying **Full-Scope Real-Time Auditing** within selected areas and processes—covering full-scope coverage, comprehensive transaction verification, and real-time monitoring—is essential for clearly demonstrating the tangible benefits of AI-Driven Audit. Quantifying Pilot successes effectively convinces both management and frontline stakeholders.

3. **Culture: Overcoming Resistance in the Internal Audit Team Through Tangible Successes**

   Alleviating psychological resistance within the internal audit team requires providing team members with direct, tangible experiences of the benefits. Use early adopters and advocates proactively to spread positive messages, while carefully engaging indifferent or skeptical individuals one-on-one, deepening their understanding and acceptance of AI integration.

4. **Organization: Small-Scale Project Team and Efficient PMO Management**

   The Pilot should launch rapidly with a compact project team. A centralized PMO (Project Management Office) will efficiently manage tasks and progress, swiftly overcoming challenges. Early engagement of international offices will further ensure smoother global expansion in subsequent phases.

5. **Skillset: Intensive Training and OJT to Quickly Build Pilot Member Capabilities**

Pilot team members should undergo focused, in-person training and on-the-job training (OJT) to rapidly enhance their practical AI competencies and consulting proficiencies. Gathering feedback from Pilot participants helps refine and improve training content, laying the groundwork for broader organizational rollout.

6. **Technology: Agile Development of an AI Auditor (Axel) Prototype**

Rapidly build a minimal-functionality prototype of the **AI Audit Platform** (Axel) through agile development, using Pilot operations to swiftly iterate improvements. Essential security measures are implemented during the Pilot, setting the stage for secure and successful large-scale deployment in subsequent phases.

LOOKING AHEAD TO THE NEXT CHAPTER: THE PILOT AS THE DECISIVE FACTOR IN AX SUCCESS

The Pilot phase represents the single most critical milestone within the broader AX initiative. Demonstrating concrete, small-scale successes at this stage builds internal confidence and positive perceptions such as "AI-Driven Audit truly adds value" or "This will significantly improve efficiency," greatly accelerating momentum toward full-scale implementation. Conversely, frequent issues or inadequate results during Pilot can severely stall or derail the AX transformation.

The secret to Pilot success lies in focused trials within limited domains and proactively sharing tangible outcomes internally. By practically demonstrating new methodologies such as full-scope auditing, comprehensive data verification, and real-time monitoring, organizations effectively reduce internal skepticism and anxiety. Such strategic actions become a powerful driver of enthusiasm—shifting organizational sentiment to "AI-Driven Audit is beneficial" and "Let's expand this further."

The next chapter—**Implement (Full-Scale Deployment)**—builds on these Pilot successes, aiming to broadly embed **Full-Scope Real-Time Auditing** throughout the enterprise. This crucial step cements the new auditing standard required in the era of **Artificial General Intelligence (AGI)**. Leveraging insights gained from the Pilot, the subsequent challenge is executing large-scale change, substantially elevating corporate governance practices. The Pilot is not the final goal; however, the experience and knowledge gained during this phase form the essential foundation that allows AX transformation to truly flourish.

A CLOSER LOOK:
BUILDING THE PRC DATABASE AS THE FOUNDATION FOR AI-DRIVEN AUDIT

In internal auditing, it is common practice to organize audit targets into a comprehensive list known as the **Audit Universe**. Ideally, an Audit Universe encompasses the entire corporate group, meticulously detailing every location, all business processes, significant risks identified within those processes, and the critical controls established to mitigate such risks. This comprehensive mapping is crucial for creating accurate and effective audit plans. However, the reality in many organizations is quite different. Often, the Audit Universe is either not developed at all or is limited to a superficial listing of the names of offices or business units.

In the era of **Artificial General Intelligence (AGI)**, organizations seriously considering the implementation of **Full-Scope Real-Time Auditing** face the unavoidable task of constructing a robust **PRC (Process-Risk-Control) database**—the equivalent of a detailed Audit Universe. The reason is straight-forward: without clearly understanding the scope of auditing coverage ("What is included and excluded?"), organizations cannot even accurately measure their current assurance coverage. Consequently, this lack of visibility signifi-cantly increases the risk of oversight and blind spots in risk management.

The primary benefit of a PRC database lies in its comprehensive inventory of all business processes, the inherent risks associated with each step, and the critical controls intended to mitigate those risks. For instance, consider a purchasing process that involves several steps: "purchase requisition → approval workflow → order placement → payment." Within each step, the PRC database identifies the associated risks (e.g., excess inventory, fraudulent orders, erroneous payments) and clearly defines the key controls required to mitigate these risks. Creating such a holistic map on a location-by-lo-cation basis involves substantial effort for initial construction and ongoing maintenance. As a result, only governance-advanced organizations currently maintain robust PRC databases. Nevertheless, as **AI-to-AI (A2A)** transac-tions increase exponentially in the AGI era, the importance of a PRC database will grow dramatically, eventually becoming an absolute necessity.

Moreover, when integrating an AI Auditor into audit operations, the PRC database serves as the essential backbone. The **AI Audit Platform** refer-ences this database as a "map," systematically verifying each control's

design adequacy (appropriateness of control design) and **operational effectiveness** (actual execution of controls). To evaluate control design adequacy, the AI automatically collects and analyzes process-flow diagrams, relevant internal regulations, and interviews with various departments, determining if the controls are properly designed. For operational effectiveness, rather than relying on traditional human internal auditors who examine limited sample transactions, an AI Auditor can perform comprehensive, real-time monitoring across all transactions. Consequently, the rate of early detection of fraud and errors improves dramatically, significantly reducing concerns related to auditors inadvertently overlooking significant risks outside their sampled transactions.

In short, the PRC database forms the foundation of effective AI-Driven Audit. By evolving the Audit Universe concept to explicitly define every location, business process, associated risks, and necessary controls, organizations can clearly visualize the comprehensive landscape of **Full-Scope Real-Time Auditing**. If your audit department is currently wondering where to begin preparations for the AGI era, we strongly recommend starting with the establishment of a robust PRC database.

Chapter 7

Implement—Enterprise-Wide Expansion of the AX Framework

—Scaling from Pilot Success to a New Organizational Normal—

INTRODUCTION: FROM PILOT SUCCESS TO ENTERPRISE-WIDE TRANSFORMATION

In the previous chapter on **Pilot implementation**, we recommended testing AI-Driven Audit in limited processes and domains, generating small yet impactful successes (**Quick Wins**) that will help to shift internal attitudes towards a positive perception of AI auditing. In this chapter, leveraging insights and confidence gained from the pilot stage, we transition to the **Implement phase**, scaling **Full-Scope Real-Time Auditing** across the entire organization.

This stage represents a pivotal moment in your organization's **AX (AGI Transformation)** journey. While the pilot tested AI-Driven Audit in selected areas, this phase involves the comprehensive deployment across all locations and processes, requiring significant transformations in your organization's structure, culture, and evaluation systems. Strong, coordinated actions across multiple fronts will be essential —including alignment with top management, coordination with global offices, and change management to reduce resistance from audited departments.

Yet, it is through successful implementation that your organization can realize the true promise of **Full-Scope Real-Time Auditing** powered by AI, dramatically enhancing the company's risk detection and governance capabilities. This chapter details key strategies from the MCOST perspectives (Methodology, Culture, Organization, Skillset, and Technology), offering actionable insights to expand pilot successes to enterprise-wide adoption.

7.1 Implementation Methodology: Rolling Out Full-Scope Real-Time Auditing Enterprise-Wide

7.1.1 Standardizing and Scaling AI-Driven Audit

During the pilot phase, we introduced **Full-Scope Real-Time Auditing** on a limited basis—for instance, conducting comprehensive checks and continuous monitoring within procurement processes or selected locations, and generating measurable successes. In the implement phase, we aim to extend this proven model throughout the entire organization with clearly defined objectives:

- **Expansion of the PRC database across all units**

  o Expand the **Process-Risk-Control (PRC) Database** developed during the pilot, capturing every location, process, and associated risk, thus achieving genuine full-scope coverage.

  o For locations or processes lacking detailed risk and control inventories, perform rapid risk assessments and progressively incorporate findings into the PRC database.

- **Standardization of continuous monitoring**

  o Extend the real-time auditing model from pilot-tested processes to all critical operations enterprise-wide.

  o Establish a new auditing framework where the AI Audit Platform continuously monitors every transaction and automatically notifies internal audit teams on the detection of anomalies.

- **Complete departure from traditional auditing approaches**

  o Move away from traditional **Rotational and Limited-Scope Auditing** and manual sampling methodologies, relegating them to supplemental or situational use.

  o Clearly define a division of roles, reserving only highly specialized areas beyond the current scope of AI-Driven Audit for targeted human review.

Implementing these measures will drastically reduce organizational blind spots and establish a robust capability for prompt detection and intervention when risks emerge. In essence, the implement phase transforms AI-Driven Audit into your organization's new normal.

7.1.2 Radical Transformation of Internal Audit Processes

The full deployment of **Full-Scope Real-Time Auditing** fundamentally alters conventional auditing practices:

- **Redefined role of risk assessments**

  o Traditionally, risk assessments focused on determining audit targets. With full-scope auditing, emphasis shifts from "where to audit" to "which AI-generated alerts to prioritize."

  o Adopt frameworks for swiftly prioritizing and addressing the most critical risks identified through continuous AI monitoring.

- **Transformation of annual audit plans**

  o Annual audit plans traditionally specified fixed audit schedules. With real-time auditing, static plans will become obsolete.

  o Annual plans will evolve into guidelines for maintaining monitoring models, updating AI audit algorithms, and dashboard enhancement strategies.

  o Reports to executive management or audit committees will become dynamic, delivered as time-responsive, actionable insights rather than fixed quarterly or annual schedules.

- **Elimination of traditional audit notifications**

  o Continuous auditing will negate the need for periodic audit announcements.

  o Regular global communications from senior executives will remind all locations about the continuous auditing practice and ensure heightened risk awareness.

- **Automation of audit programs and working papers**

  o Audit programs will be replaced by the continuously maintained PRC database, eliminating repetitive planning efforts and enhancing efficiency.

  o Audit working papers (documentation) will primarily be generated by AI audit logs and verification histories. Human auditors can then concentrate on critical decision-making areas, significantly reducing routine documentation tasks and allowing greater focus on communication effectiveness.

- **Instantaneous audit reporting**

  o Traditional paper-based or PDF reports will transition to the **Global AI Audit Cockpit (Dashboard)**, providing executives and field teams instant access to the latest risk indicators.

o This real-time capability will vastly enhance decision-making speed and quality across the organization.

In the AGI era, enterprise-wide implementation signifies a complete overhaul of audit processes, embedding the new methodologies tested during the pilot into everyday organizational practices.

7.2 Implementing Culture: Establishing an AI-Friendly Culture Across the Entire Organization

While the pilot phase primarily addresses cultural resistance within internal audit teams, the full implementation phase requires cultivating an **AI-friendly Culture** throughout the entire organization— including departments subject to audits. Since full-scale deployment will significantly increase direct interactions with AI-generated alerts among business units, resistance must be proactively managed to prevent audit processes from being ignored or undermined.

7.2.1 Reducing Resistance Among Audited Departments

During the pilot, internal auditors will have developed familiarity with the AI-Driven Audit approach. Now, audited departments must similarly embrace this cultural shift:

- **Conduct department-level dialogues**

  o Engage directly with audited departments to understand their reactions to AI alerts: "How do you perceive alerts?" and "What operational concerns arise from using AI auditing?"

  o Share positive testimonials from pilot locations emphasizing tangible benefits such as reduced errors and quicker resolution of issues, addressing and reducing skepticism.

- **Promote acceptance and mutual benefits**

  o Clarify that AI-Driven Audit benefits audited departments by enabling early problem detection, thus minimizing potential harm.

  o Foster collaborative relationships between audit teams and operational units to jointly manage and reduce risk.

- **Consistent top management messaging**

  o Leverage consistent communications from executives and board members reinforcing that AI-Driven Audit is mutually beneficial, fostering trust and cooperative attitudes.

  o By establishing an understanding that AI auditing supports departments by detecting errors or misconduct swiftly, resistance diminishes, facilitating smoother implementation.###

7.2.2 Enterprise-wide Change Management

Achieving enterprise-wide implementation requires more than technology—it necessitates an organizational mindset shift where all employees perceive AI-Driven Audit as supportive rather than punitive.

- **Broadly communicate pilot successes**

  o Utilize internal channels (meetings, intranets, internal social networks) to share compelling narratives of successful AI auditing interventions.

  o Shift perceptions from auditing as restrictive oversight to a proactive support system, highlighting concrete examples of risk mitigation and issue resolution.

- **Unified global messaging**

  o For multinational organizations, implement consistent global messaging from executive leadership emphasizing that AI auditing is beneficial, proactive, and supportive rather than punitive.

  o Regularly communicate these messages to bridge cultural and language differences, ensuring organization-wide understanding and acceptance.

- **Shift from "Monitoring" to "Support" culture**

  o Actively reposition the internal audit function from an oversight role to that of a **trusted advisor**, capable of rapidly assisting operational teams.

  o Promote successful cases where departments proactively engaged auditors for early advice, resulting in tangible business benefits.

By embedding these approaches, AI-Driven Audit will become recognized as an essential tool to accelerate business decisions and foster organizational agility, solidifying its place within your corporate culture.

7.3 Implementing Organization: Transforming the Global Audit Structure for Comprehensive Implementation

In the Pilot phase, we established small-scale **AI Audit Teams** and **Consulting Enhancement Teams**, coordinated centrally by a Project Management Office (PMO). During the **Implement phase**, reorganizing the audit structure and updating evaluation systems becomes crucial to scaling these successful initiatives across all locations and business units.

7.3.1 PMO-Led Enterprise-wide Project Implementation

The PMO, instrumental during the Pilot, gains even greater significance in the Implement phase. It takes a leading role in managing schedules, promoting AI-Driven Audit as a new standard throughout the organization, and ensuring cohesive project progression.

Launching the Global Project:

- Aggregate insights and lessons learned from the Pilot to create comprehensive Work Breakdown Structures (WBS) and roadmaps for enterprise-wide implementation.

- Clearly visualize deployment schedules for each location, prioritizing areas based on urgency and risk exposure.

Centralized Issue and Progress Management:

- Concurrently manage various tasks such as IT system integration, data migration, and human resources evaluation adjustments associated with AI-Driven Audit implementation.

- Leverage project management tools to promptly identify and address bottlenecks.

- Regularly conduct meetings with overseas teams to proactively resolve region-specific challenges.

Sharing Success Stories and Enhancing Internal Communication:

- Actively disseminate successful practices and innovations via corporate intranets, internal newsletters, and social media to accelerate deployment across locations.

- Foster a collaborative, learning-oriented culture through systematic knowledge sharing facilitated by the PMO.

7.3.2 Global Reorganization of the Internal Audit Structure

As AI-Driven Audit expands across the organization, many enterprises may consider reorganizing globally—whether adopting a centralized, decentralized, or hybrid approach. The critical factor is achieving seamless worldwide coordination between **AI Audit Teams**, who handle model operation and tuning, and **Consulting Enhancement Teams**, who deliver strategic advice.

AI Audit Teams:

- Evaluate whether centralized control from headquarters or regional teams is optimal, considering operational agility and resource availability.

- Secure high-level AI model specialists and data scientists to ensure continuous AI performance optimization.

Consulting Enhancement Teams:

- Assign consulting experts across global locations to provide immediate, culturally aligned support and implement corrective actions based on AI alerts.

- Establish effective online communication and collaboration platforms to maintain consistent information sharing with headquarters.

7.3.3 Redesigning Performance Evaluation and Career Development Systems

Full-scale implementation of AI-Driven Audit makes AI literacy and consulting proficiencies essential for auditors, demanding new evaluation metrics beyond traditional measures (such as counting identified deficiencies).

Developing New Evaluation Metrics:

- Establish KPIs such as the volume and quality of processed AI alerts, acceptance rates of proposed improvements, the effectiveness of consulting interventions, and proficiency in AI-related skills.

Integrating Metrics into Promotion and Compensation Systems:

- Directly link auditors' career progression and compensation to their demonstrated ability to transform AI-generated insights into meaningful strategic advice, thus directly contributing to business performance.

Creating Clear Career Paths from Audit to Executive Management:

- Highlight that experience with AI-Driven Audit will position auditors as future executive leaders due to their comprehensive organizational insight.

- Clearly articulate career pathways to strategic planning or international management roles, creating a talent magnet effect that strengthens audit capabilities through skilled personnel.

Implementing these measures will ensure that auditors' efforts are appropriately recognized and incentivized, further reinforcing their motivation and the attractiveness of audit roles within the organization.

7.4 Implementing Skillset: Scaling Auditor Training for Comprehensive Skill Enhancement

Whereas training during the Pilot focused on a select group, the Implement phase represents a strategic opportunity to significantly elevate the overall skillset of auditors organization-wide.

7.4.1 Effective, Scalable Training Through Level-Based On-Demand Learning

With **Full-Scope Real-Time Auditing** becoming standard, all auditors must possess basic AI understanding and consulting proficiency. Scalable, on-demand training segmented by skill level is highly effective for achieving this goal.

Introductory Course:

- Covers basic principles of AI-Driven Audit, alert management fundamentals, comparisons to sampling methods, foundational AGI concepts, and essential security protocols.

Intermediate Course:

- Emphasizes practical operational aspects, including business intelligence (BI) tool integration, data privacy, and security risk management.

Advanced Course:

- Addresses specialized topics like AI model auditing, ESG considerations, and international collaboration.
- Additionally, e-learning and video content provide flexibility, allowing auditors worldwide to learn at their convenience. Creating supplementary online forums encourages peer-to-peer interaction and shared learning.

7.4.2 Implementing Global Training and Certification Programs

Effective global deployment requires standardized training and certification processes, ensuring consistent skill development and minimizing variations across international teams.

Unified Global Curriculum:

- Implement core training modules in AI-Driven Audit and consulting universally, complemented by region-specific modules addressing local regulatory and cultural nuances.
- Facilitate the adoption of a uniform audit methodology across all locations.

In-House Certifications and Skill Recognition:

- Establish internal certifications (e.g., AI Audit Expert, Senior Consultant) through post-training evaluations or practical assessments, enhancing transparency in skill development.
- Incorporate these certifications into human resource evaluations, motivating auditors toward ongoing professional growth.

Global standardization of training enhances flexibility in team management, simplifies internal rotations, and ensures consistent audit quality worldwide.

7.5 Implementing Technology: Deploying the AI Audit Platform ("Axel") Across All Enterprise Units

In the Pilot phase, we operated the AI Auditor, Axel, as a prototype in selected areas, continuously refining its capabilities through tuning to minimize false positives and negatives. Now, in the Implement phase, we will expand this platform across the entire enterprise, establishing **Full-Scope Real-Time Auditing** as the new technological standard supporting internal audit processes.

7.5.1 Continuous Iterations Leading to the Official Release of the AI Auditor (Axel)

The prototype version of Axel developed during the Pilot phase has now undergone numerous enhancements and tuning processes. In the Implement phase, the focus shifts toward its official, enterprise-wide release, emphasizing rapid iterative development.

Agile Development and Iterative Improvements

- **Implementing enhancements through iterative sprints**: Continuously incorporate improvements identified during the pilot, such as multi-location integration, prioritization of alerts, and dashboard expansions, releasing updates in short, frequent cycles.

- **Avoiding traditional "waterfall models"**: Large-scale waterfall approaches often cannot keep pace with rapid advancements in AI technology or adapt quickly enough to changing organizational requirements.

Prioritizing Essential Enterprise-wide Functionalities First

- Prioritize the implementation of core functionalities necessary for broad operational use, such as:

  o **Real-time alerts**

  o **Anomaly detection in key business processes**

  o **Integration with the Global AI Audit Cockpit (Dashboard)**

- Optional functionalities should be implemented after receiving actual operational feedback, allowing for more efficient and relevant feature deployment.

Concurrent Updates of the AI Auditor and Audit Methodologies

- Concurrently update internal audit methodologies and conduct training alongside system development. Waiting until system completion to initiate methodological changes can significantly delay enterprise-wide adoption. It is essential to iteratively test and implement new methods in parallel with technology development.

- Through these continuous iterations, the AI Auditor will evolve into a robust system capable of covering the entire enterprise. By the end of the Implement phase, it will be ready for official deployment across almost all locations.

7.5.2 Enterprise-wide Operational Deployment of the AI Auditor (Axel)

Deploying the AI Auditor across all business locations and processes—achieving true **Full-Scope Real-Time Auditing**—requires making several significant strategic and operational decisions:

Selecting the Deployment Model: Cloud, On-Premises, or Hybrid

- Many enterprises prefer cloud solutions to handle large volumes of data; however, businesses dealing with highly sensitive transactions often retain on-premises systems.

- Increasingly, companies adopt a hybrid cloud approach after carefully considering security policies, costs, and international connectivity conditions.

API Integration and Expansion to All Locations

- Axel must integrate with ERP and related systems across various locations via APIs to collect necessary data effectively.

- PMO coordinates with each location to schedule the development, testing, and deployment of these APIs, minimizing downtime and disruption to daily operations.

Optimal Management of Large-Scale System Updates

- A simultaneous enterprise-wide replacement of core systems risks significant operational disruption; thus, a phased approach is recommended.

- PMO centrally manages the implementation schedule, prioritizing deployments in higher-risk business areas first and adopting flexible rollout strategies to minimize disruption.

With Axel operational at an enterprise-wide scale, **Full-Scope Real-Time Auditing** becomes the established corporate standard, signaling the definitive end of reliance on outdated auditing methodologies like **Rotational and Limited-Scope Auditing** or sampling-based testing. Audit committees and executive boards will gain the capability to monitor risks continuously via dashboards, promptly addressing significant errors or fraud at their earliest stages.

7.5.3 Enhancing Security, Privacy, and Regulatory Compliance

As we progress from Pilot to full-scale implementation, the volume and complexity of data handled by the AI Auditor will drastically increase. Consequently, strengthening security, privacy protection, and regulatory compliance measures becomes paramount.

Adopting Zero Trust Architecture

- Introduce a Zero Trust model to verify each access request from various locations and systems individually, minimizing internal misconduct and external cyber threats.

- In environments characterized by frequent **AI-to-AI (A2A)** transactions, strict API security reviews are essential, with mechanisms to block suspicious communications proactively.

Ensuring Compliance with International Regulations (EU AI Act, GDPR, etc.)

- Multinational corporations must meticulously assess regional privacy laws and AI-specific regulations, defining clear policies for data storage and explainability of AI models.

- Establish robust operational rules and monitoring systems to ensure that the AI Auditor's handling of personal data and sensitive commercial information fully complies with legal requirements.

Integrating Incident Response and Business Continuity Plans (BCP)

- Establish contingency mechanisms (e.g., redundancy and failover solutions) to ensure audit continuity even if the AI Audit Platform experiences outages or cyberattacks.

- Incorporate detailed recovery procedures for the AI audit systems into the broader Business Continuity Plan, enabling audits to continue uninterrupted even during major disruptions or disasters at key sites.

Implementing these measures in the full-scale deployment phase secures robust protection for real-time audit operations across the enterprise. By achieving advanced security and regulatory compliance, the entire organization can confidently leverage AI auditing, operating securely and legally across international markets.

KEY TAKEAWAYS FROM THIS CHAPTER

1. **Implement Phase: Establishing AI-Driven Audit as the New Enterprise Standard**

   Building upon successful Pilot implementations, organizations will be able to extend **Full-Scope Real-Time Auditing** to all business locations and processes, dramatically enhancing their risk detection capabilities and governance standards.

2. **Methodology: Comprehensive Audit Process Overhaul and Transition to Real-Time Model**

   Transition fully away from traditional approaches, such as **Rotational and Limited-Scope Auditing** or sampling-based testing, adopting instead a comprehensive model in which AI continuously monitors activities. The audit planning process evolves toward prioritizing critical alerts, and reporting becomes centralized around a real-time dashboard—the **Global AI Audit Cockpit (Dashboard)**.

3. **Culture: Enterprise-Wide Change Management to Foster an AI-friendly Culture**

   Promote widespread acceptance of AI-Driven Audit by ensuring all employees—including audited departments—understand that AI auditing is designed to support business improvement and timely risk mitigation. Share success stories and engage top management to reduce resistance and build a receptive organizational mindset.

4. **Organization: Global Reorganization of Audit Functions Driven by PMO Leadership**

   Scale from small teams in the Pilot phase to enterprise-wide deployment guided centrally by a Project Management Office (PMO).

Reorganize global **AI Audit Teams** and **Consulting Enhancement Teams**, updating evaluation systems and redefining career paths to reflect new audit capabilities and roles.

5. **Skillset: Enhancing Auditor Skills Through Comprehensive Training and Certification Programs**

    Enable auditors to acquire essential AI literacy and consulting competencies through structured, level-based, on-demand training and globally standardized certification systems. Integrate these new skill sets into formal evaluation frameworks, linking skills enhancement directly to career advancement and compensation.

6. **Technology: Enterprise-Wide Operational Deployment of the AI Audit Platform ("Axel")**

    Leverage insights gained during the Pilot phase to refine and fully deploy the AI Audit Platform ("Axel") using agile development methodologies. Ensure comprehensive API integration, robust security, privacy safeguards, and regulatory compliance, resulting in a stable, continuously operational audit infrastructure.

LOOKING AHEAD TO THE NEXT CHAPTER: ELEVATE—DEEPENING PROACTIVE AUDITING THROUGH CONTINUOUS IMPROVEMENT

The Implement phase transitions AI-Driven Audit from initial experiments to the corporate standard, institutionalizing **Full-Scope Real-Time Auditing** across the entire organization. At this point, traditional auditing methods—such as **Rotational and Limited-Scope Auditing** or sampling-based testing—begin to fade into obsolescence, replaced by instantaneous risk detection and adaptive auditing processes embedded within corporate culture.

However, achieving widespread deployment does not signify the end of AI auditing integration. In the AGI era, technological advances, risk environments, and business models continuously evolve at an accelerating pace. Detecting and addressing risks alone will not suffice; internal audit functions must deliver increasingly higher value to the organization.

In the next chapter, **Elevate (Continuous Improvement)**, we will explore the next horizon of auditing practices—examining how consulting proficiencies and risk management strategies can evolve to create a cutting-edge auditing model for the AGI era. With the audit foundation solidified during Implement, the Elevate phase allows the auditing organization to flourish, significantly amplifying its strategic impact.

Chapter 8

Elevate—Continuous Improvement Toward Next-Generation Auditing

—From Real-Time Assurance to Predictive, Value-Creating Insight—

INTRODUCTION: THE CONTINUOUS EVOLUTION OF AX WITHOUT AN END POINT

In the preceding chapters, we've followed a clear trajectory through **Assess (Current State Assessment)** → **Envision (Vision Setting)** → **Pilot (Pilot Implementation)** → **Implement (Full Implementation)**, gradually expanding AI-Driven Audit from limited trials to enterprise-wide adoption, ultimately institutionalizing **Full-Scope Real-Time Auditing** as the new audit standard.

However, in the ongoing era of Artificial General Intelligence (AGI) and AI-to-AI (A2A) interactions, both business models and technology evolve rapidly. If you seek merely to maintain current auditing frameworks, they can quickly become obsolete. If companies assume that "AX (AGI Transformation) of internal auditing is now complete," the sophisticated **Full-Scope Real-Time Auditing** systems they have painstakingly developed may quickly lose their relevance and effectiveness.

Thus arises the necessity for **Elevate (Continuous Improvement)**, which this chapter addresses. Elevate ensures the continuous updating of internal auditing practices to keep pace with AGI-era advancements. Moreover, it fosters a robust risk culture, enhances consulting proficiencies to support proactive management decisions, and strengthens global audit frameworks—initiatives that directly contribute to increasing corporate value. Elevate is not just the concluding step of AX; it is the foundation for an ongoing cycle of advancement.

8.1 Continuous Improvement of Methodology: Automated Updates and Enhanced Value of AI-Driven Audit

8.1.1 Continuously Maintaining an Updated PRC Database

Throughout the Implement phase, enterprises will have established the **PRC (Process, Risk, Control) Database** to facilitate enterprise-wide adoption of **Full-Scope Real-Time Auditing**. However, in the rapidly changing AGI era, new AI agents, business process revisions, mergers and acquisitions of overseas locations, and divestitures all necessitate continuous updating. The Elevate phase, therefore, emphasizes creating mechanisms that consistently keep the PRC database up to date.

AI-Driven Automated Updates

- Employ document analysis AI and log analysis AI to continuously monitor internal rules, contracts, and new business systems, automatically detecting emerging risks and control gaps.

- Human auditors review these AI-generated recommendations, approving immediate updates to the PRC database.

Such automation prevents oversights—such as failing to update the PRC database following the deployment of new AI agents—and consistently maintains the integrity of the Full-Scope approach.

Regular Data Cleansing of Obsolete Controls

- The accumulation in the database of controls that have become obsolete (due to AI advancements or process restructuring) leads to noise and reduced auditing efficiency.

- Establish regular review sessions to remove or archive obsolete controls, keeping the PRC database relevant and actionable.

With these mechanisms, the PRC database is continuously updated and cleaned, ensuring that **Full-Scope Real-Time Auditing** remains aligned with rapid business developments, minimizing risks even amid increasing A2A transactions.

8.1.2 AI Auditor's Global Risk Information Integration

In the Elevate phase, the **AI Auditor (Axel)** evolves beyond analyzing internal data to integrate global external risk intelligence into the PRC database

- **Global Regulatory Updates**

  Continuously integrate evolving global regulatory changes, such as the EU AI Act or U.S. state-specific privacy laws, automatically updating associated controls and risks.

- **Industry Fraud and Incident Monitoring**

  AI will automatically parse fraud cases or emerging cyber threats from peer companies, verifying if similar vulnerabilities exist internally.

- **Economic and Geopolitical Risk Alerts**

  The monitoring of macro-level risks—such as political instability or currency fluctuations—will enable proactive adjustments in financial controls and supply chain strategies

With global information continuously integrated, the AI Auditor will act as a forward-looking "eye for management," enabling proactive responses by the internal audit function.

8.1.3 Sustaining Full-Scope Real-Time Auditing Through Automated Updates and Data Cleansing

By implementing automated updating and systematic data cleansing, **Full-Scope Real-Time Auditing** will evolve from a mere capability to a sustainable enterprise infrastructure. Regular database maintenance and timely inclusion of new processes or regulations become key points of Elevate's strategic continuous improvement.

This ongoing mindset of endless updating must become ingrained organizational practice.

8.1.4 Enhancing the Global AI Audit Cockpit (Dashboard)

During Implement, dashboards provided real-time reporting capabilities. In Elevate, this evolves further into a sophisticated **Global AI Audit Cockpit**, enabling executives and boards to grasp an organization-wide risk profile at a glance.

- **Real-Time Visualization of All Alerts**

  Aggregates alerts and controls deficiencies worldwide into real-time visualizations (maps and graphs), allowing executives to instantly identify where risks concentrate geographically.

- **Development of Key Risk Indicators (KRI)**

  Quantitatively evaluate alerts based on indicators such as financial impact, compliance risk, or reputational damage, allowing strategic resource allocation.

- **Upgrading Dashboards to the Global AI Audit Cockpit Standard**
  Enables the management to always have the latest risk information, significantly accelerating global decision-making in an AGI-driven environment where risks evolve rapidly.

This sophisticated Global AI Audit Cockpit is critical to effective risk management and informed strategic decision-making in the AGI era.

8.1.5 External Quality Assessments to Confirm Alignment with Global Internal Audit Standards

Even as AI-Driven Audit methods mature through Elevate, it will remain essential to comply with global internal audit standards. Regular external quality assessments will maintain trust and credibility internally and externally.

- **Alignment with IIA Global Standards**

  Adhere to core audit principles such as independence, due professional care, quality assurance, and continuous improvement programs outlined by the Institute of Internal Auditors (IIA).

- **Regular External Quality Evaluations**

  Confirm that the AX methodology, including real-time monitoring, adheres to global audit standards, verifying that even radically evolved AGI-era methods remain compliant.

- **Integrating Identified Improvements**

  Act on external feedback (e.g., gaps in AI Model Auditing documentation or independence guidelines) to further strengthen AX methodologies.

Regular external validation of alignment with global standards will establish the trustworthiness and credibility of advanced AGI-era audit practices.

8.2 Continuous Improvement of Culture: Embedding AI Acceptance and Risk-Aware Culture Throughout the Organization

8.2.1 Cultivating a Company-wide Risk Culture Through Three Lines Collaboration

Effectively utilizing **Full-Scope Real-Time Auditing** in the AGI era requires deep collaboration across the three lines of defense:

business units (the first line), risk management/compliance (second line), and internal audit (third line).

- **PRC Database as a Common Language**

  Establish the PRC database as the shared risk management language across all three lines, ensuring uniformity and clarity of definitions.

- **Role of the First Line (Business Units)**

  Instill a culture of proactive risk identification and immediate corrective action, leveraging real-time PRC data for self-discovery and self-correction even before audit alerts.

- **Role of the Second Line (Risk Management/Compliance)**

  Continuously update the PRC database with emerging regulatory and technological risks and maintain regular communication with the first and third lines.

- **Role of the Third Line (Internal Audit)**

  Maintain independence while leveraging AI analytics to provide strategic advice and facilitate collaboration among all three lines.

Such integrated collaboration will become the foundation for strategic, proactive auditing.

8.2.2 Establishing AI-Driven Audit as a Business Accelerator

As **Full-Scope Real-Time Auditing** becomes normalized, perceptions of auditing will shift significantly. The real-time oversight provided by the AI Auditor will help avoid significant losses and accelerate decision-making, leading to broader appreciation of auditing's proactive value.

- **CEO and Board Messaging**

  Continuously reinforce the idea of AI-Driven Audit as an essential safety mechanism accelerating management action rather than constraining it.

- **Highlighting Success Stories**

  Regularly communicate concrete instances of the AI Auditor preventing significant losses, reinforcing internal audit's reputation as a **trusted advisor**.

- **Fostering a Positive Attitude toward Risk-taking**

  Emphasize quick recovery enabled by real-time auditing rather than striving for unrealistic zero-failure, thus enabling confident risk-taking.

Creating this positive cultural shift will transform internal auditing into a supportive safety net that encourages bold strategic initiatives, thus fueling accelerated business growth in the AGI era.

8.3 Continuous Improvement of the Organization: Positioning Audit as a Gateway to Executive Leadership

8.3.1 Strengthening Internal Audit's Consulting Role to Accelerate Proactive Audit

After implementing AI-Driven Audit enterprise-wide, and embedding **Full-Scope Real-Time Auditing** as the norm during the Implement phase, the Elevate phase further enhances internal auditing's consulting proficiencies. Leveraging daily insights and improvement opportunities provided by the AI Auditor, the audit function actively contributes to enhancing corporate value.

Standardization of Improvement Projects

- Establish templated processes for improvement projects based on risks or deficiencies detected by AI.

- For instance, standardize the workflow from **"alert → initial investigation → assigning responsible individuals → considering countermeasures → implementation → monitoring,"** enabling the audit department to swiftly act in a consultant-like manner.

Deepening Global Coordination

- In multinational enterprises, quickly share control deficiencies and fraud cases discovered at overseas locations with other regions.

- Consequently, internal audit can lead global business improvements, significantly accelerating organizational transformation.

Proactive Recommendations to Boost Revenue

- Beyond merely identifying issues, the internal audit function proactively suggests strategic improvements, such as supply chain optimization, cost restructuring, or risk assessments for new projects.

- Utilizing comprehensive data gathered from AI-Driven Audit, auditors can provide precise hypotheses and decision-making support, elevating the audit department's strategic significance.

8.3.2 Transforming Internal Audit into a Gateway to Executive Management

An internal audit function that fully integrates AX will naturally cultivate skills in AI literacy, consulting proficiencies, and global adaptability. Individuals gaining experience in this environment will emerge as strong candidates for future executive roles.

Advantageous Personnel Policies

- Create systems that make internal audit experience particularly attractive in career development, actively promoting accomplished audit members to corporate planning departments or overseas leadership roles.

- This will encourage high-performing talent to actively seek positions in internal audit, thus continuously strengthening **AI Audit Teams** and **Consulting Enhancement Teams**.

Internal Rotation Programs

- Bring young talent from other departments or overseas locations into internal audit for on-the-job training (OJT) in AI-Driven Audit.

- After a few years, these individuals can return to their home departments or regions as leaders, bridging gaps between internal audit and operational units, creating an effective talent rotation model.

Strong Alignment with Top Management

- CEOs and boards will increasingly implement recommendations from internal audit promptly, maintaining active and continuous communication between management and audit teams.

- By cementing its role as a **trusted advisor**, the internal audit function will contribute significantly to enterprise-wide innovation.

Through such organizational enhancements, the Elevate phase will transform internal auditing beyond mere oversight into a robust consulting group and executive management training institution.

8.4 Continuous Improvement of Skillset: Advancing Auditor Expertise in AI, Management, and Global Competencies

8.4.1 The Necessity for Continuous Learning

In the AGI era, AI technologies evolve rapidly, continually introducing new methods, services, and integration technologies. Hence, Elevate emphasizes an essential mindset for auditors—continuous learning.

Rapid and Unceasing AI Evolution

- AI continues advancing rapidly, incorporating self-learning systems, new algorithms, and API integrations.

- To deliver "100-fold assurance" in collaboration with AI Auditors, auditors must remain consistently updated on the latest tools, methodologies, and best practices.

Integration with Emerging Technologies (Metaverse, Quantum Computing)

- Businesses may soon operate within metaverse environments or leverage quantum computing capabilities.

- Auditors must proactively acquire knowledge about such advanced technologies, maintaining a mindset of lifelong learning.

Continuous Improvement of Learning Platforms

- Enterprises should regularly update training content and online learning platforms, ensuring auditors have optimal resources for learning about new technologies.

- Regular workshops on topics such as cutting-edge **AI Model Auditing** practices or global regulatory trends will help support auditors at a company-wide level.

Auditors should embrace the joy of continuous learning rather than feeling overwhelmed by rapid technological advancements—this attitude is crucial in Elevate.

8.4.2 Cultivating Auditors with Superior AI × Management × Global Skillsets

Critical skills for auditors in the AGI era include AI proficiency (AI literacy, data analytics), consulting proficiencies (logical thinking, business acumen), GRC expertise (governance, risk, compliance), and global adaptability. In Elevate, auditors strive to integrate these skills, becoming true hybrid professionals—masters of AI × Management × Global.

First, Specialize Deeply in One Domain

- Individuals should initially excel in specific areas, such as AI analytics, strategic consulting, or local expertise of overseas subsidiaries.

- Gradually, through practical experience and training, auditors can expand their knowledge into complementary domains.

Ultimately Becoming Fully Integrated Professionals

- Although challenging, comprehensive mastery of these skills will position auditors as highly sought-after global experts.

- Such elite auditors will become superstar auditors, significantly increasing their opportunities to advance into executive or global leadership roles.

Supporting Auditors' Growth Toward Excellence

- Enterprises can actively support professional development through targeted training, certifications, and international rotations.

- Establishing an environment where auditors naturally acquire comprehensive expertise will make internal audit attractive to top talent, further accelerating AX evolution.

The Elevate phase presents an ideal opportunity for auditors to significantly enhance their personal value, unlocking greater possibilities for internal auditing in the AGI era.

8.5 Continuous Improvement of Technology: Ensuring Trust in AI Auditors Through Ongoing Model Audits and Reliability Improvement

Even after firmly establishing **Full-Scope Real-Time Auditing** throughout the enterprise, business environments will continue to evolve rapidly in the AGI era. In Elevate, it is critical to continuously improve the AI Auditor's quality management, updates, security, and business continuity planning (BCP) to sustain operational excellence.

8.5.1 Official Operation and Advancement of AI Model Auditing

While Pilot and Implement phases tuned AI Auditor accuracy, the Elevate phase formally integrates regular AI Model Auditing into operational processes, enhancing transparency and reliability regarding AI Auditor quality, bias, and modification history.

Formalization of AI Model Auditing: Continuous Bias and False-Positive Reduction

- Institutionalize AI model validation processes—such as quarterly or monthly assessments of false positives/negatives—to continuously refine accuracy through systematic feedback loops.

- Introduce bias detection mechanisms to quickly correct disproportionate risk evaluations, ensuring unbiased AI judgments across regions and processes.

Integration of Explainable AI (XAI)

- Implement XAI capabilities to clarify reasons behind AI-generated alerts, avoiding the "black-box" phenomenon.

- Regularly include AI model audit results in audit committee and management reports, increasing transparency and reducing executive anxiety about AI decision-making.

Securing Objectivity Through External Reviews

- Regularly involve external audit firms or AI experts to review internal AI model auditing processes, enhancing objectivity and trustworthiness.

- Align auditing practices with international standards (e.g., IIA standards, EU AI Act), boosting corporate-wide compliance and public trust.

Transparency Through Audit Reporting

- Include AI model auditing outcomes in audit and management reports, clearly communicating AI accuracy, bias detection, and remediation efforts.

- This will foster internal confidence in the AI Auditor, mitigating concerns and ensuring sustained trust.

Through regular, formalized AI Model Auditing during the Elevate phase, enterprises can avoid blind reliance on AI, maintaining consistently accurate, unbiased AI auditing—critical for long-term trust in the AI Auditor as a reliable internal partner.

When an audit flags systematic bias, an independent shadow model re-runs both current and historical audit data. A second validation model may confirm any major discrepancies, after which unresolved items go to human reviewers. We cap automation at two layers, delivering reasonable assurance while avoiding an endless chain of "AIs auditing AIs." The shadow pass also highlights past decisions that now fall outside risk limits so they can be corrected or re-reported.

8.5.2 Strengthening Security and BCP for Uninterrupted Real-Time Auditing

Post-establishment of enterprise-wide **Full-Scope Real-Time Auditing**, evolving risks and regulations will necessitate continuous enhancement of security and BCP:

- **Coordination with AI Model Auditing:** As AI advances, security threats grow increasingly sophisticated, requiring regular security validations within model auditing to detect vulnerabilities promptly.

- **Expansion of Zero Trust Architecture:** Continuously update authentication, encryption, and log visualization across headquarters, global offices, and cloud environments.

- **Multicloud and Failover Validations:** Regularly conduct practical BCP drills and "chaos engineering" exercises to guarantee uninterrupted auditing operations.

- **Adapting to Emerging Regulations:** Incorporate readiness plans for future compliance needs, such as quantum-resistant encryption standards and evolving AI regulations, within regular AI Model Auditing cycles.

This continuous focus on security and BCP will ensure that internal auditing continuously delivers uninterrupted real-time assurance, positioning the audit function as a reliable enabler of confident corporate innovation in the AGI era.

KEY TAKEAWAYS FROM THIS CHAPTER

1. **Elevate (Continuous Improvement): Transforming AX into Proactive Audit**

   AX is not a one-time implementation—it will demand continuous evolution to remain relevant amid rapid changes in the AGI era. Ongoing improvement will translate directly to enhanced corporate value.

2. **Methodology: Continuously Optimize AI-Driven Audit to Build a Management Cockpit**

   Automatically update the PRC (Process, Risk, Control) database, integrating external risk intelligence to ensure it remains constantly current.

   Establish an advanced **Global AI Audit Cockpit (Dashboard)**, enabling management to immediately grasp the enterprise's risk landscape. Conduct periodic external quality assessments to ensure alignment with international auditing standards.

3. **Culture: Embed a Risk Culture Viewing Auditing as a Safety Device Accelerating Business Growth**

   Foster a culture in which the three lines of defense (business units, risk management, internal audit) proactively manage risks using a shared PRC database.

   Top management should consistently communicate a clear message encouraging employees **not to fear mistakes**, but to instead emphasize early detection and prompt corrective actions.

4. **Organization: Transform Internal Audit into an Executive Leadership Development Hu**

   Leverage alerts generated by AI Auditors to actively propose tangible business improvements, thereby enhancing contributions to corporate management.

   Establish structures making internal audit experience advantageous for promotions to executive positions, thus positioning internal audit as a leadership training ground attracting top talent.

5. **Skillset: Cultivate Hybrid Auditors Mastering AI × Management × Global**

   To cope with incessant advances in AI technology and emerging business models, auditors must maintain a mindset of continuous learning.

   Develop auditors who combine AI proficiency, strategic business acumen, and global adaptability through practical training and experience, ultimately increasing the pool of globally capable auditors.

6. **Technology: Sustainably Enhance Trust in AI Auditors Through Model Audits and Robust Security Measures**

   Formally operationalize **AI Model Auditing**, continuously reducing bias and false positives while leveraging Explainable AI (XAI) for greater transparency.

   Strengthen risk management across the enterprise through Zero Trust, multicloud operations, and comprehensive BCP, ensuring uninterrupted stability in real-time auditing.

LOOKING AHEAD TO THE NEXT CHAPTER:
AX IS CONTINUOUS EVOLUTION, AND YOU SHAPE THE FUTURE

Elevate represents the fifth phase of AX, following the four stages of Assess → Envision → Pilot → Implement. At this juncture, the primary goal is to continuously update AI-Driven Audit while significantly strengthening its consulting proficiencies to fully realize Proactive Audit. As AI-to-AI (A2A) transactions continue to evolve rapidly, this transformation should be perceived not as a threat, but rather as an opportunity to further enhance the value of internal auditing—the true essence of AX.

As outlined in this chapter, continuously updating the PRC database and fostering a robust risk culture through active collaboration among the three lines of defense will enable your entire organization to proactively manage risk, fueling innovation. Moreover, by utilizing the Global AI Audit Cockpit to maintain oversight across the enterprise—achieving a virtuous cycle of **AI-enabled risk visibility combined with human-led strategic consultation**—your organization will ascend to a new level of maturity.

Throughout this book, we have consistently emphasized that AX is not a one-time project, but rather a journey of continuous evolution. As organizations grow, global environments shift, and AI advances, the role and expectations of internal audit will inevitably transform. Yet, the framework for adapting to this constant evolution represents the core of Elevate, marking not just the culmination of AX, but the starting point for the next AX iteration.

Having explored all phases of the AX (AGI Transformation) journey, you might now feel equipped with theoretical insights and methodologies. Nevertheless, envisioning practical scenarios—anticipating real-world successes and challenges—may still prove challenging.

In the next chapter, we will provide a vivid fictional case study, illustrating precisely how one enterprise undertakes the AX journey from Assess through Elevate, clearly demonstrating the challenges overcome and milestones achieved. Learning from realistic scenarios, alongside theoretical understanding, will provide you with invaluable insights and practical guidance to apply AX effectively within your organization. We encourage you to use this case study as a reference and inspiration to shape your own organization's unique AX journey.

Chapter 9

A Case Study of AGI Transformation (AX) in Internal Audit: The AX Journey of GlobalCorp (2025–2030)

—Contrasting Fates: Companies that Adopted AX and Those that Did Not—

PROLOGUE: THE DIVERGING PATHS OF TWO COMPANIES

In early 2025, a major manufacturing conglomerate named **GlobalCorp**, headquartered in the United States, was at the peak of its market power. With more than 100 global locations, over 50,000 employees, and annual revenues exceeding $10 billion, the company stood as an industry leader. However, decades of aggressive international expansion had dramatically complicated business processes across its overseas subsidiaries. Recently, transactions driven by **AI-to-AI (A2A)** interactions had seen explosive growth, sparking growing anxiety among senior management and internal audit teams, who feared their traditional, human-driven auditing methods were no longer adequate.

In stark contrast stood **OldWays Inc.**, GlobalCorp's frequent competitor of comparable scale. Despite having similar annual revenues, OldWays' senior management stubbornly adhered to conventional auditing methods. The mindset among its leadership was firm: "Why change our audit methods? Rotational and limited-scope auditing conducted by human auditors has always worked just fine. If it ain't broke, don't fix it." Many employees quietly questioned the wisdom of continuing without preparing for accelerating AI and A2A transactions, yet organizational inertia blocked meaningful reforms.

This chapter explores the diverging fortunes of these two companies between 2025 and 2030 through a speculative narrative scenario, vividly illustrating the genuine value of internal auditing's **AX (AGI Transformation)** in the age of AGI. What were the outcomes for the company that adopted a comprehensive, AI-Driven Audit strategy, compared to the one that did not?

9.1 The Year 2025: Assess Phase—A Sense of Urgency Triggers Assessment

9.1.1 CEO Andrew's Anxiety

Early 2025. In GlobalCorp's executive boardroom, located on the top floor of its headquarters building, CEO Andrew wore an unusually grim expression, lightly striking the table with his hand in a steady rhythm. The soft thud echoed heavily, filling the room with tension.

"Do you fully understand what's happening at our overseas subsidiaries? AI agents at our locations are practically running our procurement and shipping operations by themselves, with human approvals becoming mere formalities. Essentially, our transactions are now largely AI-to-AI. While that undoubtedly boosts productivity, what if large-scale fraud is lurking unnoticed? Do you truly believe our current audit system can handle such complexity?"

The board members exchanged uneasy glances, speechless. Each recalled past scandals at overseas subsidiaries that had caused severe stock plunges, painfully aware that another incident could expose them personally to significant liability. Andrew's anxiety was rooted deeply in this stark reality.

As tension filled the air, Andrew continued softly yet firmly:

"The traditional methods—rotational and limited-scope audits, combined with sampling-based testing—simply can't keep up with these rapidly proliferating A2A transactions. Audit costs are ballooning while our coverage shrinks, potentially increasing risks. Ignoring this situation could provoke another major scandal, shaking our very foundations. We no longer have the luxury of time."

Though the board members nodded in agreement, they felt confused, unsure precisely how to proceed. Nevertheless, Andrew's speech became the catalyst, marking the very first steps toward GlobalCorp's **AX (AGI Transformation)** of internal auditing.

9.1.2 Audit Leader Sarah's Confrontation with Reality and Newcomer Alicia's Shocking Discovery

Responding to CEO Andrew's urgent call, Sarah, head of the Internal Audit Department, immediately launched a comprehensive investigation into audit coverage across the entire company.

"What is the audit coverage rate at each subsidiary? To what extent are AI-to-AI transactions covered? Could past sampling audits have missed significant issues?"

Faced with mountains of data, Sarah silently worried, wondering where to begin.

Just then, a newcomer named Alicia Davis joined the department. Alicia, fresh from university and passionate about AI, firmly believed that combining audit practices with AI could dramatically reduce risks. Despite Alicia's limited professional experience, Sarah saw promise in her enthusiasm and determination, and boldly decided to put Alicia in charge of the extensive research project.

A few days later, Alicia submitted her findings, which grimly confirmed Sarah's worst fears:

"Audit coverage per subsidiary currently stands around 10%. When considering critical control points at each location, the actual coverage drops to about 5%–6%. Our sampling methods barely scratch the surface, selecting only a handful of transactions. Practically speaking, we have no meaningful oversight of AI-agent transactions."

Reviewing Alicia's report, Sarah fell silent. The underlying severe lack of assurance behind the statistics hit her with chilling clarity. She quickly made up her mind: "I must present these findings transparently to the board and propose initiating the AX project." The vision Sarah had quietly nurtured—building an "AI Auditor"—was finally about to materialize.

9.2 The Year 2025: Envision Phase—Challenging the Envision

9.2.1 The Boardroom Presentation: Alicia Witnesses a Transformational Vision

A month later, at an extraordinary board meeting, Sarah confidently unveiled her presentation titled "Project Axel." Her materials included a specific roadmap aiming to achieve **Full-Scope Real-Time Auditing** in the AGI era.

"Currently, we barely touch A2A transactions, even via sampling. Our solution is to construct our own AI Auditor—named Axel—placing AI at the heart of auditing. Axel will enable constant monitoring across all subsidiaries and all critical risks, catching irregularities

and mistakes in real-time. Within a year, we'll initiate pilot programs in key locations, with full global deployment targeted within three years."

Sarah spoke with passion and clarity. Although some board members initially questioned the necessity of such large investments, CEO Andrew instantly expressed strong support:

"Ignoring these risks will ultimately cost us far more. Considering the damage to our corporate reputation that another crisis would cause, transitioning to AI-Driven Audit is non-negotiable."

Watching the presentation, Alicia felt excitement at the revolutionary vision yet also worried about the enormity of the project. "Can an organization of 50,000 people really transform so quickly?" Yet Sarah's unwavering conviction, combined with Andrew's resolute backing, filled her with renewed confidence. Quietly clenching her fist, she thought, "We might just pull this off!"

9.2.2 Executive Leadership Declares Proactive Audit

With formal board approval secured, "Project Axel" was quickly announced company-wide through internal communications. CEO Andrew emphasized:

"Auditing is not about policing—it's the engine that supports strategic business growth. Using AI, we'll detect risks proactively, strengthen our consulting proficiencies, and accelerate innovation. This transformation is vital to our future success."

The announcement generated substantial reactions company-wide. Some employees voiced fear ("Will AI take away our jobs?"), while others were skeptical ("Can this really work?"). Observing these mixed reactions, Alicia quietly resolved herself: "We must prepare thoroughly and demonstrate tangible success through our initial pilot."

9.3 2026–2027: Pilot Phase—Small Successes Drive Major Transformation

9.3.1 Successful Pilot in North American Procurement Processes

In 2026, Sarah and Mike, the IT department leader, carefully deliberated to identify the optimal target for their pilot implementation. They ultimately selected the North American procurement processes, reasoning that the high volume of transactions, significant risk exposure, and well-established IT infrastructure made it an ideal starting point. They understood that success here would have a powerful internal impact.

Alicia led the targeted creation of the **PRC (Process, Risk, Control) Database**. This comprehensive database captured key risks and controls in the procurement processes and included clearly defined verification procedures that an AI could interpret. Parsing through millions of procurement transactions to calibrate the database criteria was a staggering task. Initially, there were numerous complaints from the operations team: **"It's too complex," "There are too many alerts; we can't handle the workload!"** Alicia frequently struggled with the challenge: "How can we effectively reduce false positives?"

However, the atmosphere shifted dramatically a few months later when the AI Auditor delivered its first significant quick win. In just a matter of days, the AI system detected and prevented fraudulent activity totaling roughly **$500,000 per year**, astonishing senior management.

Managers, previously skeptical, murmured incredulously, **"Who could have imagined such results so quickly?"** Sarah confidently replied, **"This is the power of AI-Driven Audit. One initial success can transform everything. This is precisely the purpose of a pilot."**

Standing next to Sarah, Alicia could hardly contain her excitement: "The fraud we missed using traditional sampling methods was quickly detected by AI—this truly marks a paradigm shift."

9.3.2 Launch of PMO and Addressing Organizational Resistance

As the pilot gained momentum and success, a **Project Management Office (PMO)** was swiftly established at headquarters to manage issues and track project progress across the entire organization. Sarah took charge, while Alicia led internal communications, visiting various operational teams to continuously reinforce that **"AI auditing isn't about tightening controls; it's designed to support operations."**

As more and more concrete examples emerged—such as quickly correcting inventory discrepancies or detecting potential fraudulent invoicing at early stages—even initially resistant auditors began softening their stance. Listening to Alicia's passionate explanations, many previously hesitant colleagues admitted: **"It's actually surprisingly helpful once you start using it."** Some even noted: **"It's rare to** see a project ignite this level of passion in younger staff. Perhaps it's genuinely worth exploring."

9.3.3 Coordinating Multiple Locations and Establishing a Global Data Platform

By 2027, leveraging their success in the North American procurement pilot, **Project Axel** began expanding globally, first into European subsidiaries and then into locations across Asia. The PMO tirelessly coordinated resources, managed timelines, and addressed emerging issues. Yet, amid the daily pressures, a palpable sense of excitement about **"a truly global transformation"** energized younger team members, who approached their demanding workload with renewed enthusiasm.

Fielding inquiries from around the world, Alicia realized: "Even with cultural differences, AI-Driven Audit proves remarkably effective." Just as Sarah had anticipated, preparing for global expansion during the pilot phase significantly facilitated the subsequent large-scale rollout.

9.4 2028: Implement Phase—Company-Wide Standardization of Full-Scope Real-Time Auditing

9.4.1 Rapid Expansion of Full-Scope Real-Time Auditing

By 2028, a PMO report confirmed that **"the key data platforms and the accuracy of AI Auditor alerts are sufficiently mature for company-wide deployment."** The board of directors swiftly decided to expand **Full-Scope Real-Time Auditing** across all GlobalCorp locations.

Consequently, **Rotational and Limited-Scope Auditing** and traditional sampling-based testing quickly disappeared, giving way to a new standard built on continuous monitoring and real-time alerts via the **AI Audit Platform**. Rather than relying on monthly or quarterly reports, any indication of potential trouble was immediately visualized on dashboards, prompting instant action—a pace of responsiveness previously unimaginable within traditional internal auditing.

Reflecting on this transformation, CEO Andrew expressed genuine amazement: **"I never imagined we could audit global transactions at such high speeds and accuracy."** Turning to Sarah and Alicia, he bowed deeply, saying: **"Thank you both for making this monumental transformation a reality."**

9.4.2 Cultural Transformation and Emergence of a Proactive Mindset

With global implementation complete, perceptions of internal auditing shifted dramatically. Departments that had previously viewed audits as punitive ("I hope they don't find anything wrong with us") began seeing tangible benefits:

- **"AI flags issues in real-time, practically eliminating the need for top management to deal with problems after the fact."**

- **"Consulting suggestions from audit teams are incredibly useful in day-to-day operations."**

A growing number of employees and managers began embracing a proactive mindset: **"If AI-Driven Audit significantly reduces risk, perhaps we can confidently pursue new ventures or acquisitions."** The vision of auditing as a strategic advisor supporting proactive management decisions gradually became embedded within the company culture. Observing this change, Sarah felt a deep sense of satisfaction: **"Finally, the real value of AX is becoming clear to everyone."**

Quantitative results further reinforced success: within two years, GlobalCorp prevented over **$10 million in fraud and operational errors**, and audit coverage soared to nearly 100%, a twentyfold increase from before. While the board of directors applauded these achievements, Alicia confidently declared: "We're far from finished. AGI will continue evolving, and we can further strengthen our consulting proficiencies."

9.5 2030: Elevate Phase—Unstoppable AI Auditing Paves the Way for the Future

9.5.1 Auditing Empowers Strategic Business Growth

By 2030, GlobalCorp's **Full-Scope Real-Time Auditing** had become deeply ingrained as standard practice, including formally operationalized **AI Model Auditing**. The AI Auditor (**Axel**) continuously monitored vast volumes of **AI-to-AI (A2A)** transactions, clearly articulating why a transaction was flagged as high-risk and identifying any failing controls through **Explainable AI (XAI)**. This empowered executives with transparent, actionable insights to make rapid, well-informed decisions.

For example, when CEO Andrew or CFO Alicia asked strategic questions—"Are compliance risks manageable for our new venture in Europe?" or "How much investment will we need for regulatory compliance?"—the AI Audit Team swiftly provided scenario simulations on the dashboard, visually highlighting risk versus cost trade-offs. Decisions once limited by infrequent, backward-looking annual audit reports were now made confidently in near-real-time.

Reflecting on these changes, Alicia understood profoundly: "This is the essence of Elevate—internal auditing can genuinely become a **trusted advisor**, supporting proactive business strategy."

9.5.2 Advancing into ESG and AI Ethics, Enhancing Social Credibility

In the Elevate phase, GlobalCorp's significantly enhanced governance capabilities propelled the company into proactive engagement in **Environmental, Social, and Governance (ESG)** domains. By integrating ESG metrics into the AI Auditor—continuously monitoring factors such as CO_2 emissions and labor conditions—and systematically detecting biases through enhanced **AI Model Auditing**, GlobalCorp garnered increased acclaim from investors and society alike.

Alicia noted proudly: **"In the AGI era, meeting corporate social responsibility obligations requires swift AI-powered risk detection and mitigation. It's genuinely rewarding to contribute positively to society through auditing."**

Sarah agreed warmly: "Ten years ago, who could have imagined the audit department becoming so integral to strategic management?" Thanks to their transformative approach, GlobalCorp successfully positioned **"Proactive Audit"** at the heart of corporate growth, consistently enhancing enterprise value and earning profound trust from stakeholders and society.

9.6 A Company in Contrast: OldWays Corp.'s Struggle Without AX

9.6.1 Clinging to Outdated Audit Methods

Meanwhile, OldWays Corp., once GlobalCorp's fierce rival with nearly equal market share, stubbornly refused to embrace change. Its executive team dismissed any investment in audit enhancement, claiming, **"Spending more on audit improvements is nonsense. Our human auditors can manage just fine."** They failed to prepare for the rise of **Artificial General Intelligence (AGI)** and the rapid expansion of **AI-to-AI (A2A)** transactions. Internal audit department proposals were consistently rejected, leading to demoralization and talent attrition. As a result, the company remained largely blind to what was happening at overseas subsidiaries, where A2A transactions grew exponentially.

Each overseas subsidiary had independently implemented its own local AI agents, but the company's reliance on traditional sampling-based audits rendered effective oversight impossible. As management refused to acknowledge the growing problem, morale within the audit team deteriorated further, resulting in a damaging cycle of talented staff departures to competitors.

9.6.2 Spiraling Scandals and the Collapse of Corporate Value

By 2030, OldWays Corp. was mired in repeated large-scale scandals. Overseas operations, increasingly controlled by autonomous and rapidly proliferating AI agents, became an impenetrable black box. Fraudulent invoicing and manipulated contracts went undetected for extended periods, leading to severe external leaks that led stock prices to plunge dramatically. Investors and media aggressively questioned the delayed detection, forcing management to confess, **"Our audit processes simply couldn't keep up."**

Without sufficient funding or authority, the internal audit department could only weakly argue, **"We should have adopted AI-Driven Audit earlier."** The financial repercussions were devastating: stock prices collapsed, massive layoffs ensued, and critical business units had to be sold off. Facing enormous financial penalties, board members lamented, **"If only we had implemented AX sooner..."** but their regret came far too late.

9.7 Lessons from the Story: GlobalCorp's Success Versus OldWays' Failure

9.7.1 Keys to GlobalCorp's Success

Assess (Evaluating the Status Quo)

- Shared sense of urgency with top management, clearly quantifying gaps in assurance coverage across subsidiaries, transactions, and risks.

- CEO Andrew fully grasped the severity, setting the stage for decisive action.

Envision (Formulating the Vision)

- Clearly articulated a roadmap through **"Project Axel,"** committing to implement **Full-Scope Real-Time Auditing** within three years.

- Convinced the board through aligning risk appetite with corporate strategy, backed by a thorough analysis of investment return (ROI).

Pilot (Trial Implementation)

- Achieved quick wins by successfully detecting approximately **$500,000 in fraud** early in the North American procurement pilot.

- Significantly reduced organizational resistance, laying the groundwork for company-wide expansion.

Implement (Full-Scale Implementation)

- Rolled out **Full-Scope Real-Time Auditing** across all locations, solidifying AI-Driven Audit as standard practice.

- Revolutionized internal audit processes through continuous real-time monitoring and reporting, vastly improving risk detection capabilities.

Elevate (Continuous Improvement)

- Further enhanced proactive auditing by integrating **AI Model Auditing** and expanding into ESG domains.

- Positioned AI-Driven Audit as central to corporate strategy, consistently driving enterprise value and boosting societal reputation.

9.7.2 OldWays Corp.'s Path to Failure

- Neglected the **Assess** phase, dismissing thorough evaluations, asserting that traditional **Rotational and Limited-Scope Auditing** would suffice.

- Rejected investment in the **Envision** phase, refusing to develop a roadmap or evaluate ROI, and maintained a conservative stance.

- Did not undertake any form of **Pilot**, losing the chance to trial new technologies and demonstrate the value of AI internally.

- By skipping **Implement**, OldWays could not sufficiently manage growing risks through annual audits, eventually leading to major scandals.

- Rather than achieving **Elevate**, the company descended into an existential crisis, ultimately confronting board-level liability and severe financial consequences.

This stark contrast vividly demonstrates how internal audit reform in the AGI era profoundly influences a company's destiny.

9.8 Epilogue

Launched in 2025, **"Project Axel"** at GlobalCorp succeeded due to the passionate commitment of young Alicia Davis and the bold leadership of Sarah. After achieving pilot success in the North American procurement process and rapidly scaling through the Implement phase, GlobalCorp fully institutionalized **Full-Scope Real-Time Auditing** by 2030. Once perceived as merely a "cost center," the internal audit department had evolved into a strategic partner supporting proactive management decisions. This newfound prestige became a source of pride and inspiration for many employees, significantly increasing demand for positions in the audit department.

In contrast, OldWays Corp., by rejecting internal audit's **AX (AGI Transformation)**, struggled to cope with accelerating A2A transactions and opaque operational processes. Critical risks went unnoticed, causing catastrophic damage. Executives endured bitter regret, repeatedly lamenting their failure to act earlier. The organization suffered a continuous decline in corporate value, ultimately illustrating the tragic consequences of resistance to change.

The events between 2025 and 2030 clearly demonstrated that the ability to diligently execute each step—Assess → Envision → Pilot → Implement → Elevate—significantly influenced each company's fate. Moreover, this narrative underscores the importance of reforming all five MCOST elements (**Methodology, Culture, Organization, Skillset, Technology**) comprehensively. Implementing isolated changes is inadequate; aligning all five elements is essential to achieving effective internal auditing in the AGI era—a central message repeatedly emphasized throughout this book.

By 2030, this particular narrative reached a natural milestone. Yet the rapid evolution of AGI and A2A transactions continues relentlessly. By 2050, even more dramatic shifts are expected, prompting new challenges and opportunities. What roles might Alicia and Sarah play then, and how might the AI Auditor (**Axel**) evolve further? Indeed, the story is far from over.

Ultimately, this chapter emphasizes the critical importance of **embracing change and taking decisive action**. GlobalCorp coura-geously adopted AX and succeeded, while OldWays painfully experi-enced the cost of inaction. Despite sharing the same industry and comparable scale, their vastly different outcomes clearly illustrate the profound real-world impact of internal audit transformation. This scenario is not merely fiction; many companies today could realisti-cally find themselves at a similar crossroads.

In the next and final chapter (Chapter 10), we will summarize the journey covered so far and explore how AGI will further shape internal auditing. Additionally, we will discuss how internal audit departments can contribute strategically to corporate management and society. Maintaining the mindset that **"AX is always evolving,"** this final chapter aims to offer practical guidance for shifting your organiza-tion's internal audit toward a more proactive and strategic stance.

Now, it's your turn: Will your organization choose GlobalCorp's path— or repeat the mistakes of OldWays Corp.? Remember, the story's outcome depends entirely on your choices.

KEY TAKEAWAYS FROM THIS CHAPTER

1. **The Adoption of AI-Driven Audit Determines a Company's Future**

   In the era of **Artificial General Intelligence (AGI)**, where **AI-to-AI (A2A)** transactions are increasing exponentially, companies that embrace **AI-driven Full-Scope Real-Time Auditing** quickly detect fraud and significantly enhance their corporate value. In stark contrast, organi-zations clinging to traditional methods overlook misconduct and inevitably face existential threats.

2. **Success with AX Hinges on the Five-Step Process: Assess → Envision → Pilot → Implement → Elevate**

   Implementing change incrementally helps manage organiza-tional resistance while effectively accelerating the enterprise-wide deployment of AI-Driven Audit. Demonstrating early success (**quick wins**) during the **Pilot phase** is critical in securing buy-in from top management and employees alike.

3. **Comprehensive Reform in All MCOST Areas (Methodology, Culture, Organization, Skillset, Technology) Is Essential**

   True transformation requires more than just AI technology adoption. It demands a fundamental overhaul of auditing methodologies, cultivating a strong risk-aware culture, restructuring audit organizations, and systematically upgrading skillsets across the board.

4. **Proactive Auditing Accelerates Strategic Business Decisions**

   Adopting **Full-Scope Real-Time Auditing** significantly improves a company's ability to proactively manage risks, enabling more confident strategic decisions in new business ventures and global expansion. Consequently, the internal audit department becomes a direct contributor to enterprise value as a trusted advisor to executive management.

5. **Lessons from Contrasting Companies: GlobalCorp's Success Versus OldWays Corp.'s Failure**

   The decision to adopt **AX (AGI Transformation)** can profoundly affect a company's destiny within as little as five years. A clear commitment to transformative change, coupled with decisive action, is the surest path to corporate success.

LOOKING AHEAD TO THE NEXT CHAPTER: DEEPENING THE TRUE VALUE OF AX

In this ninth chapter, through a detailed hypothetical case study, we've vividly illustrated how successful or unsuccessful AX implementation dramatically influences a company's future. The clear contrast between GlobalCorp—successfully implementing AI-driven **Full-Scope Real-Time Auditing** to significantly boost corporate value—and OldWays Corp.—which clung to outdated auditing methods, subsequently plunging into a severe management crisis—underscores the urgent importance of adopting AX.

The next chapter (Chapter 10) consolidates the practical steps for successful AX adoption, adding further future-oriented perspectives. It explores in depth the critical question, **"How should internal auditing evolve going forward?"** Taking a long-term view extending to 2050—when advancements in AGI and accelerated A2A transactions will reshape the landscape—this chapter will outline strategies for audit departments to play more strategic roles both within corporate management and society. It covers essential enhancements, such as **AI Model Auditing**, ESG monitoring, and expanding internal audit's strategic capabilities to cultivate a higher-level, comprehensive form of proactive auditing.

For your organization to replicate GlobalCorp's success, the advanced AX strategies and implementation frameworks detailed in the following chapter will prove invaluable. Now, let's proceed to the final stage, empowering your internal audit function to firmly anchor itself at the core of corporate management and strategic decision-making.

Chapter 10
Conclusion and the Path Ahead— Taking AX to the Next Level

—Your First Step Starts Today: The Journey Never Ends—

INTRODUCTION: PROACTIVE AUDITING THROUGH AX, AND THE FUTURE BEYOND

Throughout this book, we have proposed **AX (AGI Transformation)** for internal auditing as a crucial response to the rapid changes in corporate activities brought about by **Artificial General Intelligence (AGI)**. The evolution of AI continues to make traditional auditing methodologies increasingly obsolete. In an environment where AI systems autonomously scale, executing millions— even tens of millions—of instantaneous **AI-to-AI (A2A)** transactions, internal auditors face a fundamentally new mission: **How can they proactively detect fraud and risk while providing meaningful support to executive management?**

By positioning AI not merely as an auxiliary tool, but at the core of the auditing process, internal audit can evolve into a robust **Full-Scope Real-Time Auditing** capability. This transformation shifts internal audit from a purely defensive stance to a proactive partner that substantially supports strategic management. In this concluding chapter, we revisit the insights presented thus far and outline the essential perspectives required to propel AI-Driven Audit even further into the future, exploring possibilities unique to the AGI era.

10.1 Final Recap of the AX Framework

10.1.1 Key Points of the Five-Step AEPIE Model

To effectively achieve AX, the book proposes a structured five-step framework: **Assess → Envision → Pilot → Implement → Elevate (AEPIE)**. The attempt to achieve drastic changes at one fell swoop typically encounters strong internal resistance and organizational turmoil. Following these five sequential steps ensures steady, sustainable progress. The core aspects of each phase are summarized below:

Assess (Evaluating Current Conditions)

- Conduct a comprehensive assessment of the current auditing landscape, clearly identifying specific shortcomings in assurance coverage, IT infrastructure, organizational culture, and skillsets.

- Visualize risks clearly by quantifying audit coverage rates, dependency on sampling methods, and the effectiveness of overseas auditing activities. These quantified insights become powerful motivators for senior management engagement.

Envision (Formulating the Vision)

- Define and document how **Full-Scope Real-Time Auditing** can be realized, ensuring alignment with broader corporate strategies in a detailed **AX roadmap**.

- Establish concrete KPIs and a step-by-step roadmap, securing the buy-in of top management with scenarios such as: "Within one year, key locations will pilot AX, and within three years, full-scale global AI-Driven Audit will be operational."

Pilot (Initial Implementation Phase)

- Deploy AI-Driven Audit on a limited scale (e.g., within a procurement process or a North American subsidiary) to deliver demonstrable quick wins.

- Carefully fine-tune the detection of false positives and false negatives. Early successes in detecting fraud or risk will quickly build trust, reducing internal resistance and securing support from senior management and frontline staff.

Implement (Full-Scale Deployment Phase)

- Utilize pilot-phase successes as a foundation to establish **Full-Scope Real-Time Auditing** as the corporate-wide standard auditing approach.

- Leverage a centralized **Project Management Office (PMO)** for managing the large-scale project, while simultaneously realigning evaluation systems, career paths, and organizational structures. This integration cements AI-Driven Audit as the new normal for the enterprise.

Elevate (Continuous Improvement Phase)

- Continuously advance capabilities such as AI model auditing and early-warning detection systems, empowering internal audit departments to deliver proactive consulting and strategic insight.

- Beyond operational stability of real-time auditing, auditors will deepen their advisory role in executive decision-making, ESG initiatives, and AI ethics, directly contributing to enhanced corporate value.

This carefully structured five-step approach will ensure that AX does not remain a mere theoretical exercise. Instead, it becomes a practical, deeply embedded reality within the organization, effectively driving genuine value creation.

10.1.2 Simultaneous Transformation Across MCOST

To ensure AX success, this book repeatedly emphasizes the importance of concurrently addressing five critical dimensions: **Methodology, Culture, Organization, Skillset, and Technology (MCOST)**. Reviewing each component reveals their mutual interdependencies:

Methodology

- Traditional auditing methods such as **Rotational and Limited-Scope Auditing** and sampling-based testing are no longer sufficient for comprehensive oversight of the high-speed transactions of the A2A era.

- The adoption of **Full-Scope Real-Time Auditing**, a robust PRC database, and structured **AI Model Auditing** become indispensable.

Culture

- It is crucial to address anxieties or resistance towards AI-Driven Audit, cultivating an organizational mindset that sees auditing not as a hindrance but as essential to proactively preventing risks and supporting strategic business initiatives.

- This cultural shift necessitates clear, consistent Tone at the Top messaging from senior executives.

Organization

- Build and operate integrated **AI Audit Teams** alongside specialized **Consulting Enhancement Teams**, adopting unified auditing methodologies across global operations.

- The PMO oversees the enterprise-wide project, ensuring alignment with revamped evaluation systems and clearly defined career pathways.

Skillset

- Systematically enhance skills to create Hybrid Auditors proficient in AI competencies, consulting proficiencies, Governance, Risk & Compliance (GRC) expertise, and Global adaptability.

- Continuously foster skill development through on-demand training platforms, job rotations, and cross-functional experiences.

Technology

- Deploy comprehensive **AI Audit Platforms** (such as Axel) while establishing rigorous frameworks for AI Model Auditing. Overhaul IT architectures, emphasizing cloud infrastructure, cybersecurity, and robust Business Continuity Planning (BCP).

- For multinational corporations, compliance with international regulations and data protection laws is a mandatory part of technological transformation.

Without simultaneous attention to these MCOST areas, transformation efforts risk stagnation. For example, technical deployments may fail due to cultural resistance or inadequate skillsets. AX is described as transformational precisely because it necessitates a holistic, comprehensive approach to enterprise-wide change.

10.2 Recap: Why Auditing Must Evolve in the AI Era

10.2.1 Ultra-High-Speed, High-Volume A2A Transactions and the Critical Assurance Gap

From 2030 onwards, **AI-to-AI (A2A)** transactions among AI agents are projected to occur at millisecond speeds, reaching unprecedented volumes. No matter how diligent human auditors may be, examining merely a few hundred samples during audits conducted every few years will clearly become inadequate, dramatically increasing the risk of critical issues being overlooked.

- **Limitations of Rotational Auditing**

  If a significant fraud or error occurs at a location audited only once every few years, the detection of the incident will be significantly delayed, potentially causing immense damage.

- **Sampling Methods Are Too Slow**

  When transactions scale into millions or tens of millions, scrutinizing around 25 samples inevitably leads to substantial margins of error and a high likelihood of missing critical fraudulent activities.

The only realistic solution to fundamentally bridge this **assurance gap** is to adopt AI-driven **Full-Scope Real-Time Auditing**. This approach enables continuous AI-based monitoring that instantly triggers alerts on the detection of anomalies, effectively covering the explosive growth of A2A transactions comprehensively.

10.2.2 AI and Auditing: Striking a Balance Between Proactive and Defensive Approaches

###Introducing AI-Driven Audit provides organizations with powerful tools on the defensive side, enabling swift early-stage detection of fraud and risks. More importantly, however, real-time risk visibility grants executives a sense of security that emboldens them to pursue bold, strategic initiatives without being unduly risk-averse, thereby fueling **proactive business management**.

- **Maintaining Compliance While Exploring New Ventures**

  AI auditors can provide early warnings, minimizing the risk of being blindsided by unexpected compliance breaches. This confidence will encourage executive management to execute ambitious strategies proactively.

- **Auditing as an Information Hub**

  The data aggregated by **AI Audit Teams** supports executive decision-making through analytical insights, tailored consulting proposals, and risk appetite adjustments.

Thus, internal audit in the AGI era will transcend its traditional defensive role, evolving into an essential strategic enabler of proactive business growth.

10.2.3 Maximizing Consulting Proficiencies and the Necessity of AI Model Auditing

As routine assurance tasks increasingly become the domain of AI systems, human auditors can reallocate significant resources to higher-value consulting activities. A new and crucial auditing mission accordingly arises: the ongoing assessment and oversight of AI models themselves (**AI Model Auditing**). Although AI can detect errors and fraud effectively, the deep learning algorithms driving these decisions can harbor biases or inherent flaws, underscoring the critical need for human oversight.

- **Implementing Explainable AI (XAI)**

  Embedding explanatory frameworks into AI audit platforms ensures transparency by clearly communicating the reasoning behind AI-driven alerts, thereby providing critical context for boards and executives.

- **Bias Detection and Continuous Updates**

  Human auditors must regularly assess AI models for biases such as racial, gender, or geographic skewness. Auditors then facilitate necessary model updates and retraining processes.

- **Ensuring Objectivity via External Reviews**

  Periodically engaging external auditors or specialists to independently verify AI models enhances fairness, transparency, and stakeholder confidence.

This robust audit of the AI not only elevates internal auditing to a higher level of sophistication but also reassures external stakeholders, ensuring stronger corporate governance in the AI era.

10.3 Actions for Tomorrow: How to Take the First Step Toward AX

10.3.1 Start Small, Secure Quick Wins

Implementing AX can initially seem overwhelming due to its extensive scope. Attempting an enterprise-wide launch right from the start greatly increases resistance and potential risk. An effective alternative is to adopt a **Pilot** approach.

- **Launch a Pilot in a Limited Scope**

  Select areas like procurement processes—characterized by high transaction volumes and structured data—or domains with clearly identifiable risks. Demonstrating concrete results, such as fraud detection or cost savings in a short timeframe, will solidify confidence in the value of AI-Driven Audit.

- **Communicate Pilot Successes Broadly**

  Quantify and showcase the tangible outcomes of the pilot project to gain the buy-in of top management and frontline employees. Proven successes serve as the strongest catalysts for broader organizational support.

Accumulating these quick wins will reduce internal resistance effectively, enabling a smooth transition from a successful Pilot to a comprehensive **Implement** phase.

10.3.2 Leadership Commitment and Effective Change Management

AX transcends technical and methodological reforms, representing a profound shift in organizational culture. Consequently, unwavering top management support and a strategic enterprise-wide change management plan—particularly encompassing overseas operations—are critical success factors.

- **Strong Backing from the CEO and the Board**

  Senior executives must clearly understand and support investments in AI-Driven Audit, allocate necessary budgets and human resources, and actively communicate the vision of using AI-Driven Audit to enable risk mitigation and proactive business strategy.

- **Establishing a Dedicated PMO**

  Given AX's scope—which impacts IT, HR, and global subsidiaries—a centralized **Project Management Office (PMO)** is indispensable. The PMO will ensure effective project governance, facilitate early issue detection, promote cross-departmental coordination, and swiftly escalate critical issues to senior executives.

Neglecting these aspects can lead to technological solutions becoming underutilized, increasing resistance, and ultimately causing regression to outdated manual auditing methods.

10.3.3 The Vital Importance of Reskilling

In the AGI era, auditors must be equipped with fundamental AI literacy, data analysis capabilities, and IT proficiency. Moreover, auditors will need to cultivate consulting proficiencies and a strategic executive perspective, evolving into true **Hybrid Auditors**.

- **On-Demand Training and Certification**

  Create online courses covering the core principles, operations, and anomaly detection methods of AI auditing. Providing internal certification on completion of a course enhances motivation and professional development.

- **Linking Learning with Real-World Experience (OJT)**

  Actively involve junior and mid-level staff in actual project implementations. Real-world experience gained through achieving quick wins will significantly enhance practical learning. Establish mentorship programs where seasoned auditors transfer invaluable knowledge and experience.

- **Strengthening Global Competencies**

  Effectively conducting AI-Driven Audit in overseas subsidiaries will require foreign language proficiency, local regulatory understanding, and cultural intelligence. Enhancing these global competencies through structured rotations and e-learning is essential.

Robust reskilling initiatives dramatically increase the effectiveness of AX transformations and substantially elevate organizational competitiveness.

10.4 Beyond the Horizon—AX as a Continuous Evolution

While the year 2030 serves as a significant milestone, marking the normalization of widespread A2A transactions, AI technology will undoubtedly continue its relentless advancement. By 2050, quantum computing, the metaverse, and blockchain technologies will converge, creating a world of unprecedented speed and complexity

Consequently, AX cannot be viewed as a one-time project. Instead, it must embody an iterative cycle—constantly revisiting **Assess** → **Envision** → **Pilot** → **Implement** → **Elevate**—to maintain ongoing optimization.

- **Emerging Risks and Opportunities**

  New challenges such as AI ethics, algorithmic biases, evolving international regulations, and sophisticated cyberattacks necessitate continual assessment and adaptive responses.

- **Technological Convergence and Governance**

  As metaverse-based transactions and smart contracts become prevalent, the scope of auditing responsibilities will inevitably expand, requiring pilots and controlled experimentation before broader implementations.

- **AI's Autonomous Learning and AI Model Auditing**

  In an era where AGI-level AI autonomously evolves its algorithms, the role of **AI Model Auditing** will become critically significant, necessitating that auditors be equipped with advanced and highly specialized knowledge.

Thus, AX represents an ongoing, ceaseless evolution. To ensure robust and agile corporate governance amid a dynamic future landscape, organizations must continuously cycle through the AX framework, perpetually refining their auditing practices.

10.5 Conclusion: AX as the Path to Transforming Audit into Strategic Business Support

10.5.1 The AGI Era Offers Significant Opportunities for Internal Audit

In the **AGI era**, uncertainty and complexity will increase dramatically due to the rapid acceleration of **AI-to-AI (A2A)** transactions and growing international regulatory diversity. While some may pessimistically conclude that auditing itself may no longer be feasible, this environment actually presents significant opportunities for internal auditing. Leveraging AI not only enables auditors to detect risks overlooked by traditional methods but also creates an environment where organizations can confidently embrace innovation without fearing unmanaged risks.

If internal auditors deliver robust assurance, executive teams will no longer be excessively risk-averse, empowering them to pursue bold, proactive business strategies. As a result, audit functions become critical contributors to corporate growth and transformation, generating new, strategic value for the organization.

10.5.2 The Universal Applicability of the AX Framework (AEPIE × MCOST)

The framework introduced in this book—structured as Assess → Envision → Pilot → Implement → Elevate (AEPIE) combined with simultaneous transformations across **Methodology, Culture, Organization, Skillset, and Technology (MCOST)**—is broadly applicable, regardless of an organization's size or industry

- **For Large Enterprises:**

  Complex coordination with global subsidiaries and IT departments underscores the importance of rigorous PMO oversight and strong executive commitment.

- **For Small and Medium-sized Enterprises and Startups:**

  Pilot implementations in targeted areas will enable quicker decision-making, easier realization of quick wins, and smoother expansion to other departments.

- **For Public and Non-profit Organizations:**

  The necessity of enhanced governance and compliance remains identical, with AI enabling optimal utilization of limited resources.

Rather than prematurely concluding, "Our organization cannot adopt this," start with an **Assess** phase to clearly identify issues, followed by small-scale **Pilots** to begin your AX journey effectively.

10.5.3 Auditors Who Take Action Shape the Future

Concerns about AI "taking auditors' jobs" often arise, but readers of this book now recognize this as a significant misunderstanding. Auditors collaborating effectively with AI are indispensable for organizations navigating the A2A era. As AI increasingly manages routine tasks and extensive data monitoring, human auditors can focus their energy on high-value consulting activities, such as providing strategic insights and advice to executive management.

- **Redefining Auditors' Added Value:**

  Shift away from traditional checklist-based auditing toward advanced strategic thinking, addressing complex issues like setting risk appetite and aligning risk management with corporate strategy.

- **Diversifying Career Paths:**

  Auditors equipped with AI literacy and consulting proficiencies may become future executive leadership candidates. Audit experience could soon become one of the most direct routes to understanding executive-level management.

This transformative change will be driven by your actions. Rather than passively awaiting instructions, advocate for the necessity of AX, launch small-scale pilot projects, and build momentum through success, ultimately inspiring organization-wide adoption. Both organizational and personal destinies will be significantly impacted by the question whether you passively await the future or proactively create it.

KEY TAKEAWAYS FROM THIS CHAPTER

1. **In the AGI Era, AI-Driven Full-Scope Real-Time Auditing Is Essential:**

   As A2A transactions reach millions or tens of millions instantaneously, traditional **Rotational and Limited-Scope Auditing** or sampling methods will no longer provide sufficient assurance. AI-driven **Full-Scope Real-Time Auditing** emerges as the only reliable approach for risk detection.

2. **Internal Audit's Value Is Maximized Through AI–Human Collaboration:**

   AI continuously monitors vast transaction volumes, allowing human auditors to concentrate on strategic consulting, thus balancing defensive risk management with proactive business support. Additionally, human-led **AI Model Auditing** ensures ongoing trustworthiness and transparency of AI systems.

3. **Success or Failure in AX Implementation Will Define Competitive Advantage Beyond 2030:**

   Organizations proactively implementing AX before widespread A2A adoption will benefit from early fraud detection, substantial risk mitigation, and faster decision-making, securing a competitive edge. Those failing to adopt AX risk significant corporate scandals and diminished corporate value.

4. **AX Implementation Requires the AEPIE Steps and Comprehensive MCOST Transformation:**

Successfully implementing AX requires a systematic progression through the five-step AEPIE cycle—**Assess, Envision, Pilot, Implement, Elevate**—while concurrently transforming the five dimensions of **Methodology, Culture, Organization, Skillset, and Technology (MCOST)**. Omitting even one dimension prevents AX from delivering its full potential.

5. **AX is an Ongoing Evolution, and You Are the Creator of Future Auditing:**

AX is not a one-time initiative. It requires continuously cycling through Assess → Envision → Pilot → Implement → Elevate as corporate activities and technologies evolve. Auditors who proactively drive this change hold the key to creating future organizational value.

A NEW ERA BEGINS, AND YOUR ROLE WITHIN IT

We stand at the threshold of the AGI era, an unprecedented transformation in business dynamics driven by Artificial General Intelligence (AGI). The impact on internal auditing will be equally transformative. Internal audit is no longer confined to mere "checking functions." Instead, powerful collaboration between humans and AI, coupled with the groundbreaking approach of **Full-Scope Real-Time Auditing**, will provide comprehensive risk transparency, evolving into a proactive audit function directly contributing strategic value to corporate decision-making.

Yet, no matter how innovative an idea or technology might be, it remains ineffective without people who put it into action. The agent of transformation is no one else—it is "you."

Your journey begins with the **Assess** phase. Clearly demonstrate the current assurance gaps within your organization, objectively visualizing these issues to facilitate broad organizational recognition of the need for change.

Next, through the **Envision** phase, articulate a compelling vision for the future of internal audit, clearly defining how you will incorporate AI-Driven Audit and the strategic goals your organization seeks to achieve. Engage top management and stakeholders to build consensus around this shared vision.

Then, secure small yet tangible successes during the **Pilot** phase. Demonstrable results—even in limited areas—will become powerful proof points that convert resistance into enthusiasm across departments and among executives.

During the **Implement** phase, the entire organization will experience a profound transformation. Internal audit teams, IT, HR, and many other departments collectively standardize AI-Driven Audit, embedding it as the new organizational norm.

The **Elevate** phase ultimately unlocks the true value of this transformation. By continuously conducting AI model audits and refining audit methodologies, internal auditing permanently solidifies its role as an indispensable strategic partner to corporate management.

The future remains continuously dynamic, driven by unforeseen techno-logical developments and emerging risks. By 2050, the business landscape will be more complex and dynamic than we currently imagine. However, the AX framework will equip your organization with the adaptability to leverage change as an opportunity rather than a threat.

As internal auditors, your mission is not simply to withstand the waves of change but to ride them confidently, leading your organization forward. By acting proactively, learning continuously, and driving organizational transfor-mation, you yourself create new and lasting value for internal auditing.

As you close this book, your AX journey begins. By taking the first step forward, you enter a world where internal auditing fearlessly embraces risks, accelerates corporate value, and fulfills social responsibilities—a world where proactive auditing strategically drives management toward success.

Now, step forward courageously. The very first step you take today has the potential to profoundly reshape the future of internal audit—and your own future as well.

Overview and Action Items of the AXceleration Matrix

OVERVIEW OF AXCELERATION MATRIX (MCOST / AEPIE)

MCOST / AEI2E	1. Assess	2. Envision	3. Pilot	4. Implement	5. Elevate
Overall	- Requirement definition - Identify Fit & Gap between current and ideal states	- Develop implementation plans - Obtain management approval	- Pilot implementation in selected areas - Quick wins	- Full-scale implementation across all areas - Organizational penetration	- Continuous improvement - Higher value creation
Methodology (M)	Define requirements for AI-driven, full-scope, real-time auditing in the AGI era; identify Fit & Gap	Create a roadmap for AI-driven, full-scope, real-time auditing; obtain management approval	Pilot AI-driven, full-scope, real-time auditing in selected areas	Fully deploy AI-driven, full-scope, real-time auditing across all locations and redesign auditing processes	Continuously enhance AI-driven, full-scope, real-time audit accuracy through automated AI improvements
Culture (C)	Define cultural requirements for human–AI collaboration in auditing; identify Fit & Gap	Develop change management plans for an AI-collaborative culture; secure management approval	Create success stories through pilot projects to reduce resistance to AI within the audit department	Reduce resistance toward AI throughout the organization, including audited departments, via full implementation	Continuously foster an organization-wide culture that actively embraces and collaborates with AI
Organization (O)	Define organizational requirements for effective human–AI collaboration; identify Fit & Gap	Create an organizational reform roadmap for effective AI-driven auditing; obtain management approval	Form an AI Audit Team and drive pilot projects in selected areas	Lead full implementation across all locations driven by the AI Audit Team and PMO	Position the internal audit department as a Gateway to Executive Management, activate personnel rotation, and produce management talent
Skillset (S)	Define skill requirements for auditors in the AGI era; identify Fit & Gap	Develop a talent strategy roadmap to recruit and nurture auditors for the AGI era; secure management approval	Conduct AI competency and consulting skills training, primarily for pilot project members	Conduct AI competency and consulting skills training for all audit members	Provide an on-demand learning environment enabling all auditors to continuously update their knowledge
Technology (T)	Define system environment and security requirements for AI-driven auditing; identify Fit & Gap	Define system requirements and IT investment plans for AI-driven auditing; secure management approval	Develop and fine-tune the AI Auditor (Axel); pilot in selected areas	Fully deploy the AI Auditor (Axel) across all locations; pilot AI model audits	Fully operationalize AI model audits; continuously enhance the AI Auditor (Axel)

POINTS FOR EFFECTIVE USE:

- **The vertical MCOST (Methodology, Culture, Organization, Skillset, Technology)** categories represent the five core components of AX, providing perspectives on where and how transformations occur.

- **The horizontal AEPIE (Assess, Envision, Pilot, Implement, Elevate)** stages represent the five-step process to advance AX from initial assessment through full-scale maturity.

Each bullet within the matrix summarizes key considerations and suggested actions for each stage, allowing practitioners to clearly understand "when," "what," and "which elements" to focus on to comprehensively advance AX without omissions.

Action Items for Each Step of the AXceleration Matrix

1. ASSESS

Category (MCOST)	Goals	Action Items
Methodology (M)	Define requirements for AI-driven, full-scope, real-time audits suitable for the AGI era, and identify Fit & Gap with the current state.	1) Define Requirements - Define necessary requirements for AI-driven, full-scope, real-time audits in the AGI era. 2) Confirm Current State - Confirm audit coverage. - Confirm audit cycles. - Confirm actual state of sampling-based audit methods. - Review past fraud incidents and losses. - Assess standardization level of global auditing methodology. 3) Identify Fit & Gap - Conduct comparative analysis of difference between current human-driven auditing and future AI-driven auditing methods to clarify Fit & Gap.
Culture (C)	Define cultural requirements for human–AI collaboration in the AGI era, and identify Fit & Gap with the current culture.	1) Define Requirements - Define cultural requirements necessary for collaboration between AI auditors and humans in the AGI era. 2) Confirm Current State - Confirm top management's commitment and budget policies toward AX. - Assess auditors' psychological resistance to and expectations of AI. - Confirm the current overall organizational culture. 3) Identify Fit & Gap - Conduct comparative analysis between current pre-AI culture and desired future AI-enabled culture to clarify Fit & Gap.
Organization (O)	Define organizational requirements necessary for human–AI collaboration in the AGI era, and identify Fit & Gap with the current organizational structure.	1) Define Requirements - Define necessary organizational requirements for effective collaboration between AI auditors and humans in the AGI era. 2) Confirm Current State - Confirm team structure and resources of internal audit department at headquarters. - Confirm team structure and resources of global internal audit organizations. - Assess the ratio of assurance to consulting activities. - Confirm actual audit workloads and costs. 3) Identify Fit & Gap - Conduct analysis comparing current human-centric organization and desired future organization collaborating with AI auditors to clarify Fit & Gap.

Skillset (S)	Define skill requirements for auditors in the AGI era, and identify Fit & Gap with the current skills.	1) Define Requirements - Define skill requirements necessary for auditors in the AGI era. 2) Confirm Current State - Create a skill map for internal auditors. - Confirm the current state of necessary skills for auditors in the AGI era, specifically: ① AI skills ② Consulting skills ③ GRC knowledge (Governance, Risk Management, Compliance) ④ Global responsiveness 3) Identify Fit & Gap - Conduct comparative analysis between current auditor skillsets and future required auditor skillsets to clarify Fit & Gap.
Technology (T)	Define system environment and security requirements needed for AI-driven auditing in the AGI era, and identify Fit & Gap with the current technology.	1) Define Requirements - Define system environment and security requirements necessary for AI-driven auditing in the AGI era. 2) Confirm Current State - Assess current usage of GRC tools and audit tools by the internal audit department. - Review existing internal audit department AI technology environment. - Confirm the current state of enterprise-wide data platforms and system integration. - Confirm enterprise-wide compliance status with security, privacy, and regulatory requirements. 3) Identify Fit & Gap - Conduct analysis comparing current technological environment and desired future AI-centric technological environment to clarify Fit & Gap.

2. ENVISION

Category (MCOST)	Goals	Action Items
Methodology (M)	Develop a roadmap for AI-driven, full-scope, real-time audits and obtain executive approval.	1) Identify Issues & Consider Countermeasures - Based on the Fit & Gap analysis, identify challenges to the achievement of AI-driven auditing and consider appropriate countermeasures. 2) Develop Plan - Define key KPIs to measure the achievement and effectiveness of AI-driven audits. - Develop the AX Roadmap for achieving AI-driven, full-scope, real-time audits. 3) Secure Executive Alignment - Consolidate the audit methodology reform implementation plan into an AX Implementation Plan and secure executive approval.
Culture (C)	Develop a change management plan to create a culture of collaboration with AI, and secure executive approval.	1) Identify Challenges & Consider Countermeasures - Based on the Fit & Gap analysis, identify challenges to cultivating a collaborative culture with AI and consider appropriate countermeasures. 2) Develop Plan - Define key KPIs to measure the realization of an AI-collaborative culture. - Identify tasks for fostering an AI-collaborative culture and integrate them into the AX Roadmap. 3) Secure Executive Alignment - Consolidate the culture change management plan into an AX Implementation Plan and secure executive approval.
Organization (O)	Develop a roadmap for organizational reform to enable effective AI-driven audits and secure executive approval.	1) Identify Challenges & Consider Countermeasures - Based on the Fit & Gap analysis, identify challenges to the achievement of an organizational structure in which AI auditors and humans collaborate effectively, and consider appropriate countermeasures. 2) Develop Plan - Define key KPIs to measure achievement of an effective human–AI-collaborative organization. - Identify tasks required for creating an effective human–AI-collaborative organization and integrate them into the AX Roadmap. 3) Secure Executive Alignment - Consolidate the organizational reform implementation plan into an AX Implementation Plan and secure executive approval.

Skillset (S)	Develop a strategic human resources road-map to train and recruit auditors prepared for the AGI era, and secure executive approval.	1) Identify Challenges & Consider Countermeasures - Based on the Fit & Gap analysis, identify challenges to the achievement of the desired skillset for auditors in the AGI era, and consider appropriate solutions. 2) Develop Plan - Use skill maps to define key KPIs to measure the achievement of the desired skillset for auditors in the AGI era. - Identify tasks required for developing auditor skillsets for the AGI era and integrate them into the AX Roadmap. 3) Secure Executive Alignment - Consolidate auditor reskilling and recruitment plans into an AX Implementation Plan and secure executive approval.
Technology (T)	Outline the system requirements and IT investment plan for AI-driven audits, and secure executive approval.	1) Identify Challenges & Consider Countermeasures - Based on the Fit & Gap analysis, identify challenges to building the technological foundation for AI-driven audits and consider appropriate countermeasures. 2) Develop Plan - Define key KPIs to measure achievement of the technological environment required for AI-driven audits. - Identify tasks needed to build the technological foundation for AI-driven audits and integrate them into the AX Roadmap. 3) Secure Executive Alignment - Consolidate the IT investment plan into an AX Implementation Plan and secure executive approval.

3. PILOT

Category (MCOST)	Goals	Action Items
Methodology (M)	Conduct pilot implementation of AI-driven, full-scope, real-time audits in selected areas.	1) Pilot Preparation - Partially develop the PRC database focusing on pilot project areas. 2) Pilot Execution - Partially transition from limited-scope to full-scope audits. - Partially transition from sampling-based testing to full population verification. - Partially transition from periodic rotation to real-time monitoring. 3) Quick-Win Validation - Evaluate the effectiveness of the AI-Driven Audit pilot, identify achievements, and extract issues for full-scale implementation.
Culture (C)	Generate successful pilot cases to reduce resistance to AI within the internal audit department.	1) Pilot Preparation - Conduct interviews with internal audit team members to capture insights and concerns. - Prepare effective stakeholder engagement for the AX project from the pilot phase. 2) Pilot Execution - Implement change management within the internal audit department to reduce AI resistance and establish a common understanding that AI-driven auditing is essential. 3) Quick-Win Validation - Evaluate the effectiveness of fostering a collaborative AI–human culture, identify successes, and highlight issues for full-scale implementation. - Share successful quick-win cases internally to further reduce psychological resistance ahead of full deployment.
Organization (O)	Establish an AI Audit Team and promote pilot projects in selected areas.	1) Pilot Preparation - Select a project leader and team members and initiate the AX pilot project. - Set up a PMO (Project Management Office) to centrally manage tasks and progress. - Clearly define pilot project objectives and goals, and prepare a WBS (Work Breakdown Structure) and schedule. 2) Pilot Execution - Drive AX pilot projects with centralized task and progress management by the PMO. - Ensure early involvement of overseas offices for information sharing and exchange. 3) Quick-Win Validation - Evaluate pilot project effectiveness, identify achievements, and extract issues for full-scale implementation.

Skillset (S)	Provide training in AI literacy and consulting skills primarily to pilot project members.	1) Pilot Preparation - Prepare training materials and content. 2) Pilot Execution - Conduct in-person training sessions and on-the-job training (OJT), primarily targeting pilot project members. 3) Quick-Win Validation - Evaluate training effectiveness, identify achievements, and extract issues for full-scale implementation.
Technology (T)	Develop the AI Auditor (Axel) and conduct pilot implementation with fine-tuning in selected areas.	1) Pilot Preparation - Build a prototype of the AI Auditor (Axel) with automated evaluation and real-time monitoring capabilities. - Design security, privacy, and international compliance measures for the AI Auditor (Axel). 2) Pilot Execution - Conduct pilot implementation of the AI Auditor (Axel) and verify audit accuracy. 3) Quick-Win Validation - Evaluate the effectiveness of the technological platform pilot, identify achievements, and extract issues for full-scale implementation. - Conduct fine-tuning of the AI Auditor (Axel) based on the pilot results.

4. IMPLEMENT

Category (MCOST)	Goals	Action Items
Methodology (M)	Fully implement AI-driven, full-scope, real-time audits enterprise-wide and redesign audit processes.	1) Full Implementation Preparation - Fully develop the PRC database across all areas. - Overhaul internal audit processes (risk assessment, audit planning, audit working papers, audit reporting, etc.). - Develop a Global AI Audit Cockpit (dashboard) for real-time tracking of audit activities. 2) Full Implementation Execution - Completely transition from limited-scope to full-scope audits. - Completely transition from sampling-based testing to full population verification. - Completely transition from periodic rotation to real-time monitoring.
Culture (C)	Reduce resistance to AI among all employees, including audited departments, through full-scale AI-driven auditing.	1) Full Implementation Preparation - Conduct interviews with members of audited departments to capture on-the-ground insights. 2) Full Implementation Execution - Drive enterprise-wide change management to establish the perception of AI-driven auditing as an engine of accelerated management.
Organization (O)	Lead enterprise-wide implementation driven by the AI Audit Team and PMO.	1) Full Implementation Preparation - Transition from pilot projects to launching a global AX initiative. - Reorganize the global internal audit structure to establish dedicated AI Audit and Consulting Teams. - Redesign performance evaluation systems and career paths to properly recognize and promote internal auditors proficient in AI. 2) Full Implementation Execution - Promote global AX projects, with PMO centrally managing tasks and progress. - Establish an operational framework in which AI auditors handle assurance tasks while human auditors focus on consulting services.
Skillset (S)	Provide AI literacy and consulting skill training to all audit team members globally.	1) Full Implementation Preparation - Prepare global training content tailored to varying skill levels. - Set up a global, on-demand training environment. - Establish global internal certification and skill recognition programs. 2) Full Implementation Execution - Conduct comprehensive training in AI literacy, consulting skills, and mindset training for all internal audit team members.
Technology (T)	Fully deploy the AI Auditor (Axel) across all locations and introduce model auditing of the AI Auditor on a trial basis.	1) Full Implementation Preparation - Implement security, privacy, and international compliance measures for the full-scale deployment of the AI Auditor (Axel). 2) Full Implementation Execution - Fully deploy the AI Auditor (Axel) across all operational areas. - Introduce a pilot AI Model Audit mechanism to oversee and validate the performance of the AI Auditor.

5. ELEVATE

Category (MCOST)	Goals	Action Items
Methodology (M)	Continuously improve the accuracy of AI-driven, full-scope, real-time auditing through automated, AI-based enhancements.	1) Continuous Improvement and Value Enhancement - Establish automated processes for the AI to update the PRC database whenever organizational or process changes occur. - Set up systems allowing AI auditors to automatically collect global risk intelligence and integrate it into the organization's PRC database. - Share and standardize the PRC database across the three lines of defense. - Expand and enhance the Global AI Audit Cockpit (dashboard). - Establish external quality assessments of internal audit practices to ensure alignment with global auditing standards.
Culture (C)	Continuously foster a group-wide culture that actively embraces and collaborates with AI.	1) Continuous Improvement and Value Enhancement - Continuously improve the culture of human–AI collaboration to align with evolving environmental factors and executive management needs.
Organization (O)	Position the internal audit function as a gateway to executive leadership, activating talent rotation and cultivating future leaders.	1) Continuous Improvement and Value Enhancement - Continuously strengthen the internal audit department's consulting capabilities. - Regularly refine the organizational structure to align with changes in the business environment and executive management needs. - Introduce enterprise-wide talent rotation and establish an attractive career path within internal audit. - Solidify the internal audit function's role as a trusted advisor to executive management.
Skillset (S)	Provide an on-demand training environment enabling all auditors to continuously update their skills with the latest knowledge.	1) Continuous Improvement and Value Enhancement - Regularly update training content and the learning platform to reflect environmental changes and executive management needs.
Technology (T)	Fully operationalize AI model audits for the AI Auditor (Axel), ensuring continuous improvement.	1) Continuous Improvement and Value Enhancement - Continuously improve technological infrastructure and security measures in response to environmental changes and executive management needs. - Implement Model Audits of the AI Auditor (Axel) to regularly verify accuracy and bias. - Strengthen Business Continuity Planning (BCP) for AI systems, ensuring stable and reliable AI Auditor operations.

THANK YOU FOR READING MY BOOK!

Thank you for buying and reading my book!
I'd love to connect with you and share ongoing insights and the latest developments about AI applications in Internal Audit and GRC.

Scan the QR code below to follow my IA Insight Lab,
where I regularly publish updates, opinions,
and thought leadership articles.

Scan the QR Code Here:

I appreciate your interest in my book and value your feedback as it helps me improve future versions of this book. I would appreciate it if you could leave your invaluable review on Amazon.com with your feedback.
Thank you!

www.ingramcontent.com/pod-product-compliance
Lightning Source LLC
Chambersburg PA
CBHW050113210326
41519CB00015BA/3947